PENG

Mrs Thatcher's

William Keegan has been Economics Editor of the
Observer since 1977, and Assistant Editor of the paper
since 1981. From 1976 to 1977 he worked at the Bank of
England. He has also been Economics Correspondent of
the *Financial Times*.

William Keegan

Mrs Thatcher's Economic Experiment

PENGUIN BOOKS

To my Father and the Memory of my Mother

Penguin Books Ltd, Harmondsworth, Middlesex, England
Viking Penguin Inc., 40 West 23rd Street, New York, New York 10010, U.S.A.
Penguin Books Australia Ltd, Ringwood, Victoria, Australia
Penguin Books Canada Ltd, 2801 John Street, Markham, Ontario, Canada L3R 1B4
Penguin Books (N.Z.) Ltd, 182–190 Wairau Road, Auckland 10, New Zealand

First published by Allen Lane 1984
Published in Penguin Books 1984

Made and printed in Great Britain by
Hazell Watson & Viney Limited,
Member of the BPCC Group,
Aylesbury, Bucks
Typeset in VIP Melior

Britain has, in effect, volunteered to be the
Friedmanite guinea pig. There could be no better choice.
Britain's political and social institutions are solid,
and neither Englishmen, Scots nor even
the Welsh take readily to the streets . . . There are
other advantages in a British experiment.
British social services and social insurance soften
what elsewhere might be intolerable hardship.
British phlegm is a good antidote for anger;
but so is an adequate system of unemployment insurance.

– J. K. Galbraith, *Observer*, 31 August 1980

CONTENTS

INTRODUCTION

The Conservative Party spent much of the post-war period shaking off the reputation it had acquired in the 1930s for being 'the party of unemployment'. For the majority of Tories the motives for attempting to lose that label were, no doubt, high-minded and laudable. But, quite apart from ethical or moral considerations, there was a very basic political motive at work: whatever the extreme right wing of the party might think about the usefulness of unemployment in keeping the unions at bay, about a quarter of the category of voters once known as the 'working class' traditionally vote Tory. The working class is much larger than either the upper class or the middle class. This means that something like half of the Tory vote tends to come from this section of society – known by advertising men and sociologists more familiarly these days as occupational groups C2, D and E.

It does not, therefore, take a great genius to deduce that the Conservatives are heavily dependent on the electoral support of the workers. The Tories' reputation for unemployment was considered by all sides to have been an important element in their heavy defeat of 1945. It proved a more decisive influence than their trump card at the time – namely that Winston Churchill had been such a successful and popular wartime leader. The lessons were fully absorbed by R. A. Butler and his colleagues at the Conservative research department after the war, and the unemployment label was sufficiently tattered by 1951 for the Tories to win the general election of that year. By the time Macmillan resigned in 1963 it had been torn to shreds.

How, then, did it come about that a Conservative administration after 1979 allowed the country to suffer the worst recession since the war, with manufacturing output dropping by nearly 20 per cent, and unemployment more than doubling – from 1.3 million to nearly 3.5 million in 1983? How did the party that had invested so much effort in restoring its reputation allow itself to be laid open once again to the accusation that it was the party of unemployment?

The question has wider implications than the impact on the Tory Party. More important is the impact on the country. I shall attempt to explain in the following pages first how it came about that the Conservatives came into office in May 1979 with their particular brand of economic evangelicalism, and second why things went so badly wrong – though the phrase 'why things went so badly wrong' in fact begs the question, for there is a school of thought which believes that the pain has all been necessary and that great things may result. (The real optimists, such as Walter Goldsmith of the Institute of Directors, believe they can already see such results.) While finding it difficult to accept this thesis, I have tried to be as objective as possible in exploring it – which does not preclude my drawing some conclusions.

It may help the reader to think in terms of a cartoon. At the centre of the stage is a cart-horse labelled 'the British economy and its ailments'. Attending it are the Conservative economic ministers, who are promising to cure the patient. With them they have brought a large doctor's bag labelled 'ideological panaceas'. Part One of the book is concerned with how this particular group of Tories – Margaret Thatcher and her immediate colleagues – managed to get on the stage at all; and with how their medicine bag came to be packed with its particular brand of evangelical nostrums. Part Two examines what happens to the patient when the doctors attempt to apply the cure. Everything that occurs after that is not necessarily the result of the Tory prescriptions: other developments will take place (there is a world outside) of which ramifications will penetrate the laboratory in which the great experiment is being conducted. But what the doctors do – or attempt to do – undoubtedly plays the central role.

The Bank for International Settlements in Basel referred to the 'laboratory experiment' going on in the British economy in its annual report of June 1980. On 31 August that year the distinguished American economist Professor J. K. Galbraith wrote an article in the *Observer* wrily suggesting that, if there had to be a ludicrous experiment in monetarism, what better people to inflict it on than the tolerant, phlegmatic British?

As it turned out, the disease proved to be contagious, and the whole industrialized world went into a deep recession which could only in part be attributed to the second 'oil shock' of 1979–80. Nevertheless, the effects of the recession were much more severe in this country than elsewhere. In so far as Britain's economic evangelicalism affected the world climate, its origins should be of interest to other countries also. But this is essentially a book about Mrs Thatcher's economic policies, not President Reagan's, and about how, in the author's view, they inevitably went wrong.

Part One

CHAPTER ONE

THE PRE-THATCHERITES

Tory Economic Policy before the Fall of
Edward Heath in 1974

The Tories like to think of themselves as the natural party of government. In his book *Inside Right*, Sir Ian Gilmour listed three things that the Conservatives are *not*: they are not reactionary, in the sense of resisting *all* change (they accept much of what has happened, and sometimes anticipate it); they are not a faction or pressure group, but a broadly based party; and they are not ideological. Yet on assuming office in May 1979 the Tories began at once to profess a kind of economic evangelicalism, with ideology very much to the fore. The dominant members of the party's economic team had recanted the politics of consensus which had prevailed during so much of the post-war period. They were a faction – nineteenth-century-style economic liberals. And so far from broadly accepting what previous governments had done, they made a virtue of trying to turn the clock back. How did this happen?

During the nineteenth century the Tories were responsible for many of the major social reforms. Particularly under Disraeli, they did not, like the Liberals, believe in the economic doctrine of laissez-faire, and the almost unfettered pre-eminence of the market place. They were paternalists, conscious of the responsibilities and duties of government. In modern parlance: they cared.

Or did they? After Disraeli's departure from office in 1880 the Tories went into a retrograde phase. The formation of the Labour Representation Committee in 1900 and ultimately the Labour Party is fairly convincing evidence that the Conservatives were not being all that responsive to social pressures.

The Tory Party, too, has a right wing and a left wing. The right predominated at the end of the nineteenth century and the beginning of this. But electoral reform was moving the fulcrum back towards the centre. Dependence on the working-class vote was as familiar to Disraeli as to Stanley Baldwin in the 1920s and 1930s. Baldwin was a conciliatory figure who liked to present himself as a man of the people, ironmasters though his family might be.

However, there is a tendency for the moderate wing of the modern Tory Party to wear, shall we say, blue-tinted spectacles when contemplating their past. Although men such as Baldwin may have intended to be moderate and conciliatory, that is not how they appeared to many people at the time. Indeed, it was during the inter-war period that the Tories acquired their damning reputation of being the party of unemployment – a reputation which contributed to their losing the 1945 election.

The right wing of the party is widely considered to have displayed characteristically insensitive attitudes towards the unemployed in the 1920s: the way in which the application of the means test aggravated social tensions is part of the nation's folklore. But the principal cause of the party's poor reputation was the unemployment itself. And this, it was widely felt during the post mortem, was not so much the result of the deliberate will of the party, as of the application of mistaken economic policies. After all, unemployment was also high under the ill-fated Labour administrations of the time.

During the period 1933 to 1939 the British economy emerged from the deep depression of earlier years, and grew quite rapidly. But the south fared better than the north, and the pre-war recovery is symbolized by the housing and industrial estates which sprang up on the arterial roads into London. The building and domestic appliance industries were busier than the old heavy industries of the north, which waited on the boom in the closing years of the decade. During the 1939–45 war, when all except essential factories and businesses were turned over to the war effort, the economy was fully employed.

Under the wartime coalition, it was rightly considered essential that at least some of the government's intellectual resources be devoted to plans for the economy in peacetime – in particular, to plans for keeping the people as near fully employed as possible, to avoid the waste and social misery of the inter-war period. The majority of men could not, in peacetime, be kept in the armed forces indefinitely.

By now it was recognized that there had been two major mistakes in the economic policies of the inter-war period. The first was the overvalued exchange rate adopted in the run-up to the return to the Gold Standard in 1925. The second was the old-fashioned attempt to balance the budget and conduct rigorous monetary policies when the economy was already underemployed. The two were closely connected, and it is worth dwelling on them, because the mistakes of the inter-war period furnish us with uncanny portents of the Thatcher years.

'Sound money' and 'balanced budgets' are ideals and concepts rooted in right-wing mythology. The Bank of England's official historian, R. S. Sayers, pointed out that during the 1920s the Bank used to preach that 'an uncorrected budget deficit is the root of forced increase in the supply of money and depreciation of the currency'. 'We must balance the budget' is one of those slogans that sounds like common sense. But as the American economist Paul Samuelson once said, 'it takes the most uncommon sense and wisdom to know just which part of the filing case of muddled notions that men call common sense is relevant to a particular problem'.

The essential contribution of the great economist John Maynard Keynes was to point out that what seemed to hold good for the economics of the household – the balanced budget – was not necessarily appropriate for the conduct of the financial affairs of the nation. If, during a recession, everybody 'cuts back' in order to balance his household accounts, the result will be a further fall in spending, and hence in orders from suppliers and factories, and hence in employment. What sounds prudent for the individual – spending less or saving more – may have disastrous effects for society at large, and thus for the individuals who end up unemployed. One of the favourite words in economic theory was 'equilibrium'. Keynes and his followers argued that an economy might well attain a position of equilibrium; however destructive were economic policies, output might not go on falling indefinitely; but this equilibrium need not necessarily be – almost certainly would not be – at full employment.

Given this diagnosis, the Keynesian prescription, which gradually won the intellectual and political argument, was that the government could and should intervene to stabilize economic activity and employment. It must increase its own spending – new roads and buildings gave work to construction companies; this in turn brought jobs to suppliers of materials, and plumbers; the need to furnish houses brought extra orders to the furniture and refrigerator firms; and so forth. The government could also precipitate economic recovery by cutting taxes, or raising unemployment and welfare payments. In the latter case, the route by which the government helps the private sector is more direct, but it is evident that both higher public spending and lower taxes act in the same direction.

Keynes's *General Theory* was not published until 1936, but his essential insights and ideas were part of public debate from the late 1920s, although not fully accepted until war came. Which brings us to the second major economic policy error of the 1920s: the overvalued exchange rate.

If the British economy at that time did not have a natural tendency towards full employment, that was one problem. If, furthermore, governments were mistakenly applying the policies of 'household economics' in a way which only served to aggravate the depression, that was another. But if, on top of all this, British industry was also struggling with the handicap of an uncompetitive exchange rate, then the swamp was deep indeed.

It is worth at this point quoting Sir Keith Joseph – a man who is to figure prominently in this book in connection with the economic evangelicalism which captured the Tory soul after 1974. In 1976 he said:

In Britain, after the human and economic blood-letting of the First World War, we tried to go back overnight to pre-war normality as seen through rose-tinted spectacles, ignoring the economic disruption caused by war and the long overdue restructuring the economy needed in any case.

The self-deception was symbolized by the decision in 1925 to restore the pound sterling to its post-war gold parity, to 'look the dollar in the face' in spite of all that had transpired since 1914, repeating the mistake made a century earlier against Ricardo's warnings. This ensured that the depression would reach England sooner, last longer, go deeper and undermine belief in the self-regenerative powers of the economy.[1]

The belief of Sir Keith and others in the self-regenerative powers of the economy was going to play an important role in the Conservatives' approach to economic policy after 1979. So, once again, was the impact of the overvalued exchange rate on these self-regenerative powers – an over-valued exchange rate with uncanny echoes of the policy which had caused such devastation in the 1920s. So, too, was the application of 'household economics' to the country at large.

But we are leaping ahead. When the wartime coalition made its plans for the post-war world it accepted the goal of full employment. The level of employment was not going to be left to the whims and vicissitudes of the unfettered market place: it would be achieved, it was hoped, by the pursuit of Keynesian economic policies.

The lesson of the need to avoid an overvalued exchange rate – which Keynes and like-minded officials had indeed tried to preach, to no avail, in the early 1920s – had been learned, but partly unlearned. Thus, after a devaluation in 1931, the exchange rate had been allowed to drift up again later in the decade. The pound ended the war in 1945 where it had started in 1939, at $4.03, compared with $4.80 when Britain went back to the Gold Standard in 1925, and $3.50 to $4 in the early to mid 1930s. Exchange rate policy immediately after the war, however, was not as inflexible as it had been in the 1920s. The inevitability – not to say desirability – of a more competitive rate for the pound was soon accepted, and it was devalued from $4.03 to $2.80 under the Labour Chancellorship of Sir Stafford Cripps in 1949.

The Tories made plenty of rude noises about the horrors of rationing, other controls and nationalization during the two Attlee administrations of 1945–51. They also had their fun criticizing aspects of the welfare state. But for all the propaganda against 'socialism' they broadly accepted the Labour legacy when they returned to power in 1951.

The Conservative promise in the 1951 election campaign was to 'set the people free'. Forces were already moving in that direction – there had been the 'bonfire of controls' ignited by the then President of the Board of Trade, Harold Wilson, in 1949 – and the Tories continued the process. As incomes rose during the post-war boom, people began to put by more of their earnings. This could, in theory, have prompted a repeat of the problems of the 1920s – 'excessive saving', or too much 'household economics'. But the Tories were able to combine Keynesian insights with political expediency, and to lower taxes to keep the economy moving and unemployment low.

The vogue word for the economic policies of the 1950s was 'Butskellism' – derived by the *Economist* from the names of Hugh Gaitskell (Labour Chancellor of the Exchequer at the beginning of the decade) and R. A. Butler (Tory Chancellor after him). Labour had been headed away from 'socialist' policies under Attlee's leadership – and, interestingly enough, also by the TUC. The Conservatives accepted the welfare state, the nationalization of much of basic industry (though they denationalized steel), and the commitment to full employment. Butler himself, first at the Conservative research department and later as Chancellor, was a middle-of-the-road, 'consensus' politician. His successor as Chancellor – and later the man who beat him to the leadership – was Harold Macmillan. Macmillan had been deeply affected by the pre-war unemployment in Stockton-on-Tees, his constituency. He was a Keynesian from the late 1920s and never allowed his colleagues or his officials to forget the commitment to full employment. It was towards the end of the 1950s that he coined the phrase 'You've never had it so good' – or rather, that is the phrase which Fleet Street put into his mouth, and which has lingered on. His precise words, at a garden fete in Bedford in 1957, were: 'Let us be frank about it. Most of our people have never had it so good.'

The country was sufficiently contented with its growing prosperity during the period 1951–64 to re-elect the Tories twice, increasing their majority on each occasion. There was precious little economic ideology – governments merely did their best to deliver the goods. When inflation became a more obvious problem in the early 1960s – i.e. it rose from 2 per cent to 4 per cent a year – it was the Tories who initiated bodies such as the National Economic Development Council, where government, employers and unions could discuss economic problems and the outlook, and at least attempt to put the public interest above – or on a par with – their own narrower interest.

The economic evangelicals who came into the ascendancy in the Tory Party in the late 1970s were to question the achievements of earlier administrations – both Labour and Conservative. Indeed, they blamed current problems on the expansionist policies of those earlier years. Politicians in the fifties and sixties had naturally been reluctant to dissociate themselves from any praise for their contribution to economic well-being. It was all part of the game that politicians on both sides were inclined to promise too much, and exaggerate their contribution to the march of progress. There was nothing new in that. (The most serious note of dissent was struck in January 1958, when the Treasury team of Peter Thorneycroft, the Chancellor, and his junior ministers Enoch Powell and Nigel Birch resigned over the Cabinet's refusal to implement some public expenditure cuts. This was shrugged aside with yet another famous Macmillan phrase: 'A little local difficulty.')

But the joint-party commitment to full – or at least high – employment policies was nonetheless very important. True, there were basic underlying factors contributing to economic growth and prosperity – the force of technological progress, the entrepreneurial spirit, and so on; but these had been present after the First World War too. A major difference between the two periods was the existence of the Keynesian consensus after 1945.

The basic understanding during those years was that governments would aim at full employment but that, in the favourite automobile metaphors of the time, there would be a 'touch on the brake' if the economy showed signs of moving too fast and 'overheating' – the classic signs of which were inflationary pressures and a deteriorating balance of trade and overseas payments. Conversely, the government would put 'a foot on the accelerator' if the economy was slowing down too much.

During the 1960s there was indeed an acceleration of inflationary pressure, and consequently a reappearance, in much milder form, of that economic curse of the twenties, the overvalued exchange rate. The Wilson administration of 1964–70 at first made the familiar mistake of trying to preserve a high exchange rate, but was eventually, in November 1967, forced to bow to the inevitable and devalue the pound from $2.80 to $2.40. The sixties also saw the first efforts at the more formal incomes policies which were to prove so politically explosive in the seventies, and against which Mrs Thatcher and the economic evangelicals were to react so vehemently. Incomes policies were seen by the Keynesian establishment as a supplementary weapon in the battle against inflation, since some two-thirds of employers' costs were, on average, accounted for by their wage bills. Because worries about inflation were likely to make policy-makers reach for the brake – and hence affect employment – the greater the moderation that was shown in wage claims and awards, the easier it was to reach that goal of full employment.

By the 1960s, then, Keynesian economic stabilization policies were taken for granted. But if the country's economic success under Butskellism was much more apparent than in the comparable period after the First World War, the urge to do better was nevertheless very powerful. A common criticism of the way economic policy operated was encapsulated in complaints about 'stop-go'. Since Keynesian policies were 'stop-go' almost by definition – it was not for nothing that the metaphors about the brake and the accelerator were so widely used – this seems a little harsh in retrospect. 'Stop-go' was, after all, preferable to the 'stop-stop' of the 1920s – and, as we were to see, of the early 1980s.

But just as Britain had fared relatively badly during the general world recession of the twenties, she was not doing quite so well as other countries in the boom. It was the desire to share in the even greater prosperity of our European neighbours that provided the economic motive for the succession of attempts to enter the Common Market.

Despite the considerable achievements of the British economy under Butskellism – low inflation, low unemployment, and a rapid increase in the average standard of living – dissatisfaction with the country's economic performance grew in the early 1960s. Thus in the 1964 election Labour were able to campaign on the slogan 'Thirteen wasted years of Tory misrule'. Labour made much of its putative ability to run the economy more efficiently, and Harold Wilson uttered vague references to the 'white-heat of the technological revolution'. Whatever the validity of the Labour slogan, it certainly did not work to their disadvantage in the campaign.

The Tories had had a good run, and the electorate's desire for a change might have been decisive however strong the other factors. But there *was* another factor acting against the Conservatives' chances in 1964 – and, many of them thought, militating against their hopes of being returned to power in future years. This was the popular impression of their lack of economic competence under their leader, Sir Alec Douglas-Home. Sir Alec was a man who made no secret of his lack of facility with economic matters, at a time when the economy was being seen increasingly as the central political issue. This 'thirteenth Earl of Home' had emerged as Prime Minister in 1963 when Macmillan resigned because of ill-health.

Both the manner in which Home emerged, and the fact that he emerged, offered useful political capital to Labour. This led to the rise of Edward Heath, who was going to become a controversial figure in the Tory Party in prime-ministerial office and after, and, very unwittingly, to pave the way for the rise of Margaret Thatcher and the economic evangelicals.

The intricacies of the Tory leadership struggles have filled many volumes. Our concern here is strictly with their relevance to the formulation of economic policy and the ascendancy of Thatcherism. But a brief digression on the battles of the 1950s and 1960s should assist understanding of subsequent events.

There are certain obvious qualities that leaders require; certain specific characteristics appropriate to political leaders; and certain even more specific requirements for the leadership of the Conservative Party. In his book *Conservative Leaders* Sir Nigel Fisher lists: courage; first-class mind; application; ability to communicate and persuade; understanding of people; power of decision; good political judgement. In addition one must never forget the basic folklore requirement of any candidate: 'He must be in the right place at the right time, saying the right things to the right people.' The sifting process can be taken one stage further: the candidate must want the job, and he must be acceptable – or not unacceptable – to all sections of the party.

R. A. Butler failed to succeed both Eden, in 1957, and Macmillan, in 1963, even though he was the most obvious candidate. Both failures are an endless source of fascination and controversy, not the least intriguing aspect being the behaviour of Macmillan towards Butler on both occasions. But two major questions stood out: did Butler really want the job badly enough, and was he acceptable to the right wing of the party?

This is fascinating terrain. Butler and Macmillan, more than any other politicians, were responsible for the changes and policies which made it possible in post-war years to claim that the Tories were a party of the centre, a 'consensus' government. However, as Nigel Fisher points out, 'Butskellism, though agreeable to some of us, was much disliked by others as an erosion of Conservative principles.' Macmillan led from well to the left, but knew instinctively when to make right-wing speeches. 'It would have been more difficult to reconcile the right wing of the party to Butler than for the left wing to accept Macmillan, the author of *The Middle Way*.'

The requirement in practice that a candidate be acceptable, or at least not unacceptable, to all sides must tend to favour the time-honoured compromise candidate. One of Sir Alec Douglas-Home's problems in 1963–65 was that although he was the compromise candidate to whom the inner cabal resorted in order to keep out Butler, he was not acceptable to the left wing of the party – or, at least, not for long. This was dramatically illustrated by the refusal of Iain Macleod to serve under Home. (It was not just the left of the party who were offended. Enoch Powell, too, refused to serve.)

Although the Conservative defeat in the 1964 election after thirteen years in office could not be attributed entirely to Home, it soon became apparent in both Commons and country that Sir Alec's anachronistic style was not a match for Harold Wilson. The fear grew among Conservatives on all sides that their 'natural party of government' might be doomed to many years of unnatural opposition unless their leader stood down. Sir Alec withdrew gracefully in July 1965. The 'customary process of consultation', under which a Tory leader traditionally emerged, had by now been recognized to be much too traditional, and a new electoral system had already been devised. The first election for the Tory leadership took place. And Edward Heath was sufficiently popular at that time to be elected by his parliamentary colleagues as a 'meritocratic' challenge to the meritocratic Harold Wilson.

The selection of Douglas-Home, as Macleod's resignation testified, had taken place behind the backs of the Tory left. The new electoral procedure would ensure that all factions in the party had their say. But it was also to lead, ten years later, to a new electoral procedure, for removing Tory leaders. And, by a curious twist, it was going to open the door to a right-wing leader. For there is a left wing in the Tory Party; a right wing; and a solid centre. The right – which is ostentatiously in evidence at the party conferences – would put many moderate Tories off voting Conservative forever, just as the left wing of the Labour Party repels so many of its natural supporters.

Macmillan had been masterly at pursuing consensus economic policies while making the appropriate noises in the right quarters. Edward Heath, with a two-year interval, in effect became his heir. In choosing Heath, the Conservatives were trying to restore their shaken spirits with a leader who could take on the then redoubtable Harold Wilson on his own ground. Much was made at the time, and after, of the 'new image' of the Tory leadership, of how Heath was the first lad from a grammar school to lead the party, and so on.

Heath had made his reputation first as Chief Whip, then as the minister who did his damnedest to negotiate British entry to the EEC until the veto by President de Gaulle. In the early period of opposition in 1964–65, he was generally considered to have done well in fighting the Labour Finance Bill – a role which was to bring Margaret Thatcher to the timely attention of her fellow Tories some ten years later.

Heath's campaign was successfully conducted by Peter Walker, assisted by many others; Iain Macleod, the hero of the Tory left, threw his weight behind Heath when he decided not to stand himself. Macleod's view, according to Fisher, was that Heath would make a stronger, tougher leader than his rival Reginald Maudling. Duncan Sandys, of the Tory right, took the same view. Unlike the case of Margaret Thatcher's rise to the leadership ten years later, the election of Heath brought no cries of 'foul' or 'accident'. As with Disraeli, a century earlier, the party establishment were prepared to endorse a very different mould of leader if they thought the time demanded it.

But when the Conservatives chose Heath they were certainly in a hurry. He had, as it were, rocketed to stardom. But he had not held one of the senior posts – Chancellor, Foreign Secretary, Home Secretary – considered milestones on the route to the summit. And this lack of experience was hardly going to work to his advantage. At the time Harold Wilson commented with some prescience: 'He's a splitter. If you're not on his side you're against him. He will split the party, as Gaitskell split the Labour Party.'

During those opposition years of the mid and late 1960s Heath tried to modernize the Conservative organization. There were allegedly gulfs between the leadership and the back benches; the parliamentary party and the constituency parties; the constituency parties and the electorate. The party at large would, he hoped, become more socially representative after the events that led to the unhappy reign of the thirteenth Earl. In view of the role he was to play in later events, it is noteworthy that Edward du Cann (a Maudling supporter), who had been quoted as saying that Heath's election would be 'awkward for me', was removed by Heath from the chairmanship of the party in 1967.

Heath brought a managerial style to the Tory leadership. There were study groups, weekend conferences, and active preparations for government. There was much talk of a 'quiet revolution'. During these years the right wing of the party was able to make its voice heard, but probably ended up with an exaggerated view of its influence. It was encouraged in this delusion by Harold Wilson, who dubbed the recrudescent right wing 'Selsdon Man', after the hotel in Surrey where the Shadow Cabinet met early in 1970.

Heath had been a founder member in the early 1950s of the Tory One Nation Group in Parliament. He was in the true Disraeli tradition, and much more wedded to maintaining the structure of the welfare state than the right wing seemed to realize. He dismissed calls for cuts in the social services and other wild right-wing suggestions as 'a return to the 1870s', i.e. before Disraeli's path-breaking administration. The Heath emphasis was on improving the efficiency of the economy – structural changes in government, and sensible reforms in trade union legislation.

Because of the Heath / Macleod commitment to the welfare state, there were not going to be wholesale reductions in taxation and public expenditure. Economies would be made when possible in the latter; and the perennial Tory ideal of improving efficiency via 'incentives' would be achieved by changing the structure of taxation. Mr Iain Macleod, the Shadow Chancellor, said in 1969: 'In order to achieve a vital economy taxation must be cut. But let us be quite clear what that does and does not mean. It does not mean that by international standards the percentage of income tax taken in the UK is above average. On the contrary, it is below average: it does mean that we tax the wrong things in the wrong way.' But as David Butler and Pinto-Duschinsky pointed out in their book on the 1970 general election,[2] it was easier on the hustings and door-steps to explain that taxation was too high than that it was the wrong sort; it was too complex a thought that one measure substituted for another might produce economic growth. 'Shadow Cabinet spokesmen therefore tended to use rhetoric far simpler than their proposals and compensate for rejecting the views of laissez-faire radicals by using their language.'

Language is not unimportant in politics; and not everybody in the population has access to the inner workings of a Prime Minister's mind. People at the time – including senior civil servants – had the impression that the Heath administration in the early phase was much more right-wing than had apparently been intended. Heath had not yet, of course, had the time to acquire the experience and wisdom which were to mark him out as a statesmanlike international figure of the 1980s: Heath the Younger, in a hurry to get things done, flirted with some of those right-wing tendencies he was to abhor so vehemently when they recurred, nearly a decade later, in the premiership of Margaret Thatcher.

Some outward signs of this were apparent in the faithful-rousing speech of Heath's first Secretary for Trade and Industry, Mr John Davies, when he told the party conference in the autumn of 1970: 'We shall not prop up lame ducks.' The 'lame duck' phrase certainly captured the headlines. No doubt behind it lay a more sophisticated approach – an understanding that some ducks might be irreparably lame, and others, given the right treatment, would be able once again to stand on their own webbed feet. But the impression of a less caring approach was undoubtedly fostered. Some attributed this to the tragic loss of Iain Macleod, who died a month after the Tories won in June 1970 and he had been appointed Chancellor. 'This was', says Fisher, a bitter blow to the new administration and a serious loss to the party and the nation. Especially after his death, the government approach appeared to many of us to be more right-wing than that of any Conservative Cabinet since before the war. We appreciated that Heath wanted to fashion a tougher, more competitive society, but some of the side effects were awkward and not always well handled.

This aspect of the early Heath years is important in helping us to understand the motivation of the Thatcher /Joseph /Howe policies that were to emerge in 1979. There were more parallels between the 1970 /71 Heath period and the Thatcher years than have often been acknowledged in subsequent debate. But there were also crucial differences. The differences were to prove significant in the 1979 administration: but so were the parallels, because the parallel policies were largely abandoned by Heath Mark Two. And it was the belief that they were wrongly abandoned which was to induce what hostile critics would regard as a fatal obstinacy in the subsequent Thatcher strategy.

It will be useful at this stage to bear in mind the distinction between economic policy at macro and micro levels. 'Macro', as the word implies, is concerned with 'the big picture' – for example the role of fiscal and monetary policy in promoting full employment. 'Micro' covers a multitude of areas, from the economics of housing subsidies and agricultural support to the rights and wrongs of government help for industry. Much of the thrust of the Heath administration's early years seemed to be applied to these micro areas, in the hope of improving the efficiency of the economy.

In a kind of no man's land between micro and macro issues stands the vexed issue of trade union reform. The Wilson administration of 1964–70 tried – and failed – to introduce legislation ('In Place of Strife') to make the unions behave more responsibly. The Heath administration tried too, with its Industrial Relations Act. Each failed miserably. The Amalgamated Union of Engineering Workers (AUEW) boycotted the Heath government's Industrial Relations Court, and that was, as it were, the end of the Act.

The significance for economic policy of these various incursions into the no man's land of trade union reform has always been vague. Some proponents saw a magic future in which trade union behaviour and attitudes improved on the shop floor (a micro issue), leading to improvements in productivity, and more 'responsible' wage bargaining, making policy at the macro level incomparably easier – there would be less need, for example, to resort to deflationary policies, or even incomes policies, if there was virtually no wage inflation to start with.

But of course there was. The Conservatives had abolished the Labour Prices and Incomes Board, after making the usual hostile noises about incomes policy that seemed de rigueur for both Conservatives and Labour Parties when in opposition. But wage inflation was accelerating again in 1970–72, possibly in reaction to the squeeze on incomes experienced during Roy Jenkins's Labour Chancellorship in 1967–70.

The Heath administration had not arrived in office with any deflationary plans at the macro level; there was not, for instance, any parallel with all the hopes invested in control of the money supply in 1979. But as inflation accelerated they found themselves consciously or unconsciously relying on the familiar deflationary brake to slow the economy down. In the words of a Treasury official at the time: 'We do have a counter-inflation policy: it's called rising unemployment.'

Thus there was a strategy at the micro level, and the government drifted into one at the macro level. But within two years both of these strategies were countermanded.

The micro strategy ran up against the government's unwillingness to allow such an important company as Rolls Royce to go bankrupt when it ran into trouble. And the resistance of the workers at Upper Clyde Shipbuilders to closure gave rise to a telephone message from the Chief Constable of Glasgow to No. 10 Downing Street that he could no longer be responsible for public order if the shipyard should be closed. These incidents contributed to the famous U-turn made by the Heath government.

Upper Clyde was important at both micro and macro levels. Edward Heath became very concerned about the trend of unemployment in general. The man who had been a founder member of the Tory One Nation Group found the unemployment trend morally disturbing. And the picture of a Britain in which unemployment was rising, production stagnating, and large companies failing – not all of them manifestly lame ducks – hardly accorded with his central vision of an efficient, dynamic Britain about to take its rightful place in the European Economic Community.

The deflationary policies into which the government had stumbled were never an end in themselves. When they did not seem to be working – when they appeared, on the contrary, to be aggravating the country's basic economic problems – Heath did not make the mistake of regarding them as sacrosanct. He simply decided that, if they were not promoting that wider objective, they would have to be changed. The Heath U-turn, therefore, was about means rather than ends. From improving efficiency, reforming the unions, and changing the structure of government – all in a difficult deflationary environment – the emphasis switched to achieving economic growth more directly. It was as if, in his management style, Heath had walked into the boardroom and said: 'The demand for that product isn't too good. Let's try something else. It's the profits we're really interested in.' The unions would not cooperate over industrial relations legislation? All right, let the government cooperate with the unions, as Willy Brandt – the West German Chancellor – pointed out to Heath was done in Germany. There was therefore a retreat from no man's land too.

Heath wanted to get unemployment down and to see the economy expanding. If unemployment could no longer be used as a counter-inflationary weapon, then he wanted a voluntary incomes policy. If the unions still felt too bitter about the earlier attempts to curb their power to cooperate in a voluntary incomes policy, then that policy would have to be statutory. If the unions were worried that the ambitious target for prices in the latter phases of incomes policy was a threat to their living standards, then their request for a cost-of-living protection clause would be granted. It was a U-turn at both the micro and macro levels of economic policy-making. Lame duck companies were propped up. Monetary policy was relaxed: low interest rates were introduced to encourage businesses to invest in new plant and machinery. Fiscal policy was relaxed: there were cuts in taxation and increases in public spending – indeed the floodgates previously holding back public spending were deliberately opened wide, and almost any pet development scheme that could be justified as creating jobs was dusted off the shelf.

The aim was expansion at almost any cost, with an amazingly high official growth target of 5 per cent per annum between the years 1971 and 1973. Every other major aspect of economic policy was subordinated to this end. An impressive economic recovery *was* achieved, but from Edward Heath's point of view to little avail. After a series of misunderstandings and blunders, the Conservative Prime Minister who had done so much to court the unions fell early in 1974 in that no man's land of British labour relations at the hands of the miners. An attempt to make the miners an exception to the requirements of the incomes policy broke down. The miners struck over pay – they were in an even stronger position than usual because of the worldwide energy crisis. Heath went to the polls on the issue of who governed the country – the Conservative government or the miners; and the country decided against the Conservative government.

In considering what was to come later under Mrs Thatcher's administration, the importance of the final two years of the Heath government can hardly be stressed enough. The man who had staked everything on a 'dash for growth' had been rejected in humiliating circumstances, on an electoral battleground at least partly of his own choosing. The climate was ripe for those in his own party who wished to make an assault on his leadership or on his policies; or on both.

REFERENCES

1. 'Stranded on the Middle Ground?', Centre for Policy Studies.
2. D., Butler and M. Pinto-Duschinsky, *The British General Election of 1970* (1971).

CHAPTER TWO

'THE HI-JACKING
OF A POLITICAL PARTY'

Sir Keith Joseph, Margaret Thatcher and the Rise
of the Economic Evangelicals in 1974–75

The Conservative parliamentary party dismissed Edward
Heath ignominiously from the leadership within a year of
his having lost the February 1974 election on the issue of the
miners' strike and 'Who governs the country?' The consequences of his summary dismissal were to reverberate
throughout the party and the country for years to come. His
removal was the proximate cause of the rise of Mrs Thatcher
and her band of economic evangelicals. 'It was,' says one
dissident minister, 'no less than the hi-jacking of a political
party.' It was, suggested Sir Ian Gilmour, the day the Moonies
came to Westminster.

The dismissal of Heath was a long-drawn-out, agonized
and traumatic affair, not all of whose details are relevant to
this book – not all of whose details are yet available. In
examining what is important for economic policy in what
Julian Critchley described as 'The Peasants' Revolt' we
should bear several background points in mind – points
which will come into the foreground later. One is that
feelings about the affair are still so bitter that it is almost
impossible to have an objective discussion with people who
took either side. Another is that it is too naive to argue on the
line 'the dismissal of Heath meant the rise of monetarism' or
'the monetarists removed Heath in order to change the course
of British economic policy'.

Again, the whole issue has become so emotive and cloudy
that we must beware how labels such as 'monetarist' are
used. I shall argue that even though it is meaningful to say
that the Conservative Party – or at least, its economic policy
– was captured by one faction, that one faction was itself a

coalition of various interests, some overlapping, some not. I make no apology for using the term 'economic evangelicals' to describe this coalition. It seems to me to connote reasonably accurately the kind of religious fervour Mrs Thatcher and her colleagues brought into the economic debate and to be consistent with the unashamedly 'low church' aspects of her position.

What followed Heath was the ascendancy of an economic ideology. Believers had the common view that they were right about their diagnosis of the failings of the British economy and the policies hitherto applied to it, and that they knew the revealed truth about what should be done to correct the putative crisis. They differed in the degree to which they concentrated on the purely economic issues, such as productivity and cures for inflation, and on wider issues connected (or not) with economic matters, such as their vague concepts of 'liberty' and 'freedom'. They also differed on the appropriate cure to be applied to the sick patient, and the degree of confidence they had that their cure would be efficacious. And some were just pure chancers – seizing their opportunity, and going along for the ride.

There was, as we shall see, nothing new about their ideas either. It was just that their time had come. Monetarism, for instance, which turned out in the end to mean many things to many men, was essentially an economic philosophy which specifically purported to cure inflation. It seems a reasonable hypothesis that monetarism was much more likely to gain political adherents at a time when inflation was accelerating towards 25 per cent per annum than in, say, 1957–58, when it was heading for 1 per cent, and three Treasury ministers resigned because Macmillan and his Cabinet would not allow them to cut public spending any further in line with monetarist doctrines.

It also greatly facilitated the rise of the economic evangelicals that the conventional politicians, officials and economists did not appear to have an answer to the problem of inflation – or, if they did, it was an answer that seemed less than complete. Monetarists argued that inflation was a purely economic problem, and that all it required was the appropriate economic solution. More specifically, monetarists believed that inflation was at all times a monetary phenomenon; it would not occur, or occur to such an extent, they argued, if the growth of the money supply was kept under proper control.

This of course begged the question that inflation was a purely economic problem susceptible of a purely economic solution. The conventional economic policy-makers had been inclining more to the view that, at least as manifested in modern Britain, inflation was a societal or behavioural problem: competing groups of workers, bidding for extra slices of the national cake, were the principal movers of inflationary forces. Hence the growing emphasis on incomes policies, which are an attempt to influence people's behaviour over wage claims. This leads us to another begged question: because the inflation problem was present and manifest, the evangelicals argued that previous or existing policies were inappropriate. This was a great leap from the assumption, equally plausible, that they were appropriate but had been, wilfully or no, misapplied; or that they were necessary but had so far proved insufficient.

One further factor helpful to the rise of economic evangelicalism, as we shall see, was this: whether or not conventional policies were appropriate, whether or not they had been misapplied, the conventional economic establishment was in any case in a vulnerable, not to say debilitated condition in the 1970s. Things were certainly not working as they should, or as the textbooks implied that they should. The inflation that began under Heath and continued to accelerate under the next Labour administration led to such traumatic events in 1976 that the economic establishment was not in good enough psychological shape to fight the ideologies now in the ascendant.

Before tracing how the economic evangelicals grew to be so powerful, we should distinguish the main branches of the movement. One, popularly referred to as monetarism, was the belief that the cure for inflation lay with controlling the growth of the supply of money (notes and coins in general circulation, and bank deposits of various kinds). The second was the right wing – 'thinking' and 'unthinking': the unthinking right wing believed that cutting public spending, bashing the poor and so on was a laudable activity in itself; the thinking right wing believed such things needed to be done because the level of public spending was a threat to liberty and to economic performance. This school was much impressed by an argument put forward by two Oxford economists, Roger Bacon and Walter Eltis,[1] that there was a causal connection between the growth of the public sector and the weakness of the private or 'market' sector of the economy. The Bacon and Eltis thesis caught the fashionable tide of the time, although it received something of a jolt when critics subsequently pointed out that the majority of the jobs lost to the private sector in recent years had been among males in manufacturing industry, whereas the jobs gained in the public sector were largely among females in the service industries. The latter group could not obviously have been robbed from manufacturing – unless, that is, they had changed sex in the process.

The third branch of the economic evangelical movement was the 'household economics' branch. Worshippers believed that the country, like the household, should always balance its books; and that borrowing was somehow sinful. This branch scorned Keynes and all his works, whether or not they had ever read them or understood them. Although they managed to gain all sorts of intellectual adherents, they were the economic equivalent of the flat earthers, or those who opposed Copernicus and Galileo for arguing that the earth went round the sun. Ironically, they did not even seem to understand that the typical household did not balance its books in the way they imagined, but took out mortgages from a building society, and bought furniture and electrical appliances on credit. Nor did they appear to appreciate that borrowing from banks, and the credit mechanism generally, is the life-blood of the typical firm or business.

The fourth branch was perhaps the most important branch of all: the disillusioned Keynesians. These were the men who argued with varying degrees of intensity and despair that Keynesian policies were misconceived, no longer efficacious,

even a hoax. Demand management to achieve full employment was a chimera. It only worked by driving the economy
to higher and higher levels of inflation. It was in the end a
threat to democracy itself.

Each of these branches will be explained in more detail
later. For the moment it is important to emphasize that
branch one – monetarism – had been around as a minority
view for years, but was regarded as being on the lunatic
fringe (the American economist Paul Samuelson had
described the leading monetarist proponent, Milton Friedman, as the 'eighth or ninth wonder of the world, depending
on how you score the Grand Canyon'). Branch two – the right
wing, thinking and unthinking – is always with us, but,
again, was a minority that the leaders of the Tory Party had
kept well under control in economic matters. Branch three
– household economists – tended to be a standing joke
during the heyday of the pursuit of Keynesian full employment policies in the 1950s and 1960s. And, by definition,
branch four, the disillusioned Keynesians, did not make their
views felt until they thought the creed had had its heyday.

There were two basic requirements for economic evangelicalism to take off in Britain. One was the reinforcement of
branches one, two and three; the other was a power base.
The most natural source of reinforcement was branch four –
the disillusioned Keynesian school. It would also be no mean
assistance to the burgeoning movement if, like the disillusioned and converts throughout the ages, the new recruits
were zealous, energetic and wholeheartedly devoted to their
new cause. It would also help if the atmosphere in which
they propagated the reborn faith was one of what Whitehall
officials described to me as 'eclectic agnosticism' – worry
that the tried and trusted policies were running into trouble;
willingness, on the part of a certain opportunistic element in
the economic policy machine, to try anything, particularly if
it would further their own careers, particularly if their elders
were psychologically battered.

At this stage we have to distinguish two separate but
related paths taken by the ideas which were to become so
important to British economic policy at the end of the 1970s.

One is the route through the Tory Party; the second is the route through the economic policy machine and, indeed, an important section of the Labour Party during the period 1974–78. Travellers on each path, it will be seen, were able to catch frequent glimpses of the other. The base camp for monetarist and right-wing economic policies in Britain had been established back in the 1950s, with the founding of the Institute of Economic Affairs. It was, in theory, independent of political parties and the preacher of no particular economic policy (over the years it had certainly published plenty of work by non-monetarists and non-right-wingers); but the general emphasis was clear to all and sundry. A typical apologist for the IEA would say there was nothing extreme or evangelical about the organization: it had simply concentrated on basic market economies when Keynesians – in the IEA's view straying far from the ideals of the great man himself – had wandered from the true path. The IEA has always lauded the virtues of the price mechanism and the uninhibited market place and has published work calling for market forces in such diverse fields as radio, university education and health. (One title was: 'The Price of Blood: an economic study of the charitable and commercial principle.') Conversely, it has always been opposed to controls such as prices and incomes policies, and to government intervention, except on lines approved by classical nineteenth-century 'liberals' – e.g. one has to have armies to defend the uninhibited market place, and roads for them to march on; these will probably be best provided by the public sector. The welfare state and free education hold little appeal for such people, who would ideally like to charge for everything, expand private medical insurance schemes and the like.

The IEA's faith in the virtue of the market place puts it in the neo-classical school of economics. It will be recalled that Keynesian policies were a breakaway from classical economics, questioning the assumption that equilibrium of the economy would be achieved at anything like full employment. Keynesians therefore preached government intervention to assist the achievement of full employment. In the process they may well have contributed to a fashionable swing in favour of what even they, looking back on it, might regard as an excessive degree of government intervention – an attempt, one might say, to keep the bathwater as well as the baby. The IEA and its adherents served a useful purpose as watchdogs over excessive (and possibly un-Keynesian) Keynesianism. But Keynesians would have argued in the 1960s that, given their head, the IEA would happily have the economy back in a position where the baby and the bathwater were once more in jeopardy.

What happened in the 1970s was that the IEA was given its head – or, rather, that a sufficient number of influential and ultimately powerful people came round in varying degrees to its point of view. The apotheosis of the IEA undoubtedly occurred when its director, Ralph Harris, was given a peerage in Mrs Thatcher's first honours list.

The influence of ideas and ideologies can be compared to small branches of wood thrown into a mountain stream. They are carried along for a time; they get stuck; they may never get any further; or they may be caught by a waterfall and sent hurling down to the people below. Even then, they may never be perceived by more than a handful.

The most proselytizing of the American monetarist economists – Milton Friedman – had arrived at his views well before the 1970s. British economists were aware of them, and the academic journals contained vigorous debates. But the IEA was the first organization to publish Friedman's monetarist views in semi-popular form in Britain. The basic theory was the ancient quantity theory of money: that money, like anything else, is subject to the laws of supply and demand, and if the government creates excess supplies of it, its value will go down – i.e. inflation will result. Friedman argued that in the case of the US, at least, changes in the growth rate of the money supply were as good a guide as anything else to subsequent variations in the growth of output. But on the whole he argued that variations in the growth of the money supply were not particularly good at explaining subsequent movement in output, employment and so on (the 'real economy') – it was difficult to get either the timing or the magnitude of the effect right (which is saying quite a lot – or, alternatively, very little). What was indisputable, he argued, was that previous changes in the money supply could explain, after a time lag (again, uncertain in its length), subsequent changes in the inflation rate.

Friedman argued that in any case the effect of changes in the money supply on the real economy was transitory. This left him with two basic propositions: one, leave governments to try and reduce imperfections in the market place (monopoly in both big business and the unions), because governments can do little successfully in their attempt to 'fine tune' the economy; two, in macro economic policy, let governments confine themselves to doing what is within their control, namely, aim at a moderate and stable growth of the money stock. By controlling the money supply governments would keep inflation under control. By helping the market place to work – so that the price mechanism and competitive forces should prevail in the market for money (including foreign exchange), goods and labour – governments could help to reduce the 'natural rate of unemployment' – the rate of unemployment consistent with a stable (preferably low) rate of inflation.

This was the essential Friedman message to Britain in 1970. It was not taken seriously by the economic establishment. It was ridiculed by the Cambridge economist Nicholas Kaldor, who posed the question whether the surge in retail sales just before Christmas was caused by the accompanying rise in the money supply. Bank of England economists – the men as close as anyone to the money printing process – could find no explanation of the wage inflation explosion of 1969–70 in the previous run of money supply figures.

British Keynesians had always found a close link between wage increases and subsequent increases in the average price level – i.e. the rate of inflation. Friedman argued that trade unions could not cause inflation – although, through excessive wage demands, they could price some workers out of the market and cause unemployment. Only central banks could cause inflation. Keynesians also felt that, although they had certainly had their problems, they had not done too badly over the years with their demand management policies.

Thus the Friedman message fell on deaf ears in 1970. The money supply did not rate a mention in the Conservative manifesto of that year, nor did Sir Keith Joseph or Margaret Thatcher make any fuss about it in the Cabinet in 1970–74. Indeed, more references were made to it by Labour. During the Labour government's travails with the International Monetary Fund in 1968–69, the Chancellor, Roy Jenkins, had had to pay some attention to what he described as this 'arcane' concept from Chicago – in order to please his creditors. A reference was made to a 5 per cent target for monetary growth in the 1970 Budget. After that the British government tried to give the money supply a decent burial.

There were some lonely voices among the Tories complaining of the rapid growth of the money supply after mid 1971 – during the period when the Heath administration was making its 'dash for growth'. The voices were those of Enoch Powell, John Biffen, Jock Bruce-Gardyne and Terence Higgins (who was actually Financial Secretary to the Treasury under Edward Heath and Anthony Barber). Growing concern about the rate of monetary growth was expressed in the City of London – notably by the stockbrokers W. Greenwell in the monthly financial bulletins edited by Gordon Pepper.

I would argue that a crucial role in the ascendancy of monetarist thinking in Britain in the early 1970s was played by the press. The principal economic commentators of both the *Financial Times* and *The Times* during that period – Samuel Brittan and Peter Jay – were disillusioned Keynesians. They were both struck by the combination of the acceleration of the rate of money supply growth and inflation under the Heath government, and both were avowedly influenced by Friedman (see their columns *passim* at the time). They transplanted the Friedman doctrines to Britain, but were more than mere messengers. Their discovery – or rediscovery – of Friedman coincided with the evolution of their own view that demand management was not working as supposed in Britain; there was no longer a choice between price stability and employment – the country was experiencing a period of higher unemployment and higher inflation.

Brittan did some work on the unemployment figures and argued – along with others – that they were not quite what they seemed, and that for a variety of reasons a higher level of unemployment was probably here to stay.

The essential message was that inflationary financial policies were being pursued in the name of full employment, and they contained the seeds of their own destruction. Brittan wrote:

Orthodox demand management has been based on the view that governments have the power to fix the amount of unemployment at a politically chosen level by monetary and fiscal policy. The most fundamental of the 'monetarist' contentions is that governments do not have such powers. The minimum sustainable level of unemployment is, on the contrary, determined by the functioning of the labour market. Attempts to push the unemployment percentage below this sustainable level will lead not merely to inflation, but to an increasing rate of inflation and ultimately to currency collapse.[2]

Jay argued that trade unions raised wages, thus causing unemployment by pricing some people out of jobs, and that governments expanded the money supply in order to reduce unemployment so that they could get re-elected. This led to ever-accelerating inflation, and posed a threat to the democratic process itself.

Academic monetarist economists were also fertile during these years; although they had less direct influence on politicians than journalists such as Brittan and Jay, they had frequent contact with the latter. The monetarist movement in Fleet Street interacted with the sister movement in the City, and the ministers who were subsequently to carry out Mrs Thatcher's economic policies concede that they were influenced by it. But the monetarist movement was sufficiently specialized for many Tories to have claimed to me subsequently that they had never heard of monetarism until after the ascendancy of first Keith Joseph and then Margaret Thatcher in 1974–75. 'We voted against Ted, and then we found we had monetarism,' is the way this group put it.

The flow of monetarist ideas in Britain would seem to have started in the academic world, moved on to Keynesian economic commentators in Fleet Street experiencing their first pangs of disillusionment, and finally reached what was to become an influential caucus of politicians. (The only famous politician to have preached a form of monetarism before the tide turned was Enoch Powell.) To change the metaphor of the flow of ideas, one must distinguish between the odd monetarist breeze, and the effect of monetarist ideas when they became a powerful force, and swept up a number of influential people in their path.

We have seen that the monetarist message was available from across the Atlantic during the 1960s – Friedman was then based in Chicago, which had a long association with the quantity theory of money, stretching back to the turn of the century. Peter Jay was certainly referring to monetarism in his columns in the late sixties, and recalls receiving – indeed provoking – letters attempting to put him right from across the Atlantic. But these were flirtations. With unemployment close to a million in early 1972, Jay had not yet arrived at that turning point where monetarism was fully acceptable and demand management was rejected. Indeed, writing of the Heath /Barber expansionary budget in spring 1972, Jay said: 'As to the need to avoid a purely ephemeral spurt leading to another stop, that is the language of the 1960s and has little application to a situation in which the economy is operating at least 7.5 per cent below its full employment capacity.'

A year later, in spring 1973, Jay was questioning whether the recovery – indeed boom – could be sustained, and during 1973–74 his views, and those of the editor of The Times, William Rees-Mogg, became progressively more monetarist. A similar conversion was taking place in the mind of Samuel Brittan at the Financial Times, although, unlike The Times, the Financial Times did not also espouse monetarism whole-heartedly in its leader columns.

A forceful monetarist academic presence in London at the time was Professor Harry Johnson, who managed physically as well as intellectually to bring monetarist ideas across the Atlantic by simultaneously holding academic chairs at the London School of Economics and Chicago University. In

1969 Johnson helped to set up the Money Study Group, which became a forum for monetary debate. Professors David Laidler and Michael Parkin of Manchester University embarked in July 1971 on a research programme on inflation which led them to conclude that monetarism could explain much about British economic problems, and that incomes policies had little effect in reducing inflation. The small but growing band of British monetarists made disturbing predictions about the likely course of inflation in November 1972 (Economic Radicals, 'Memorial to the Prime Minister'). Alan Walters, subsequently Mrs Thatcher's economic adviser in Downing Street in the early 1980s, was also a pioneering British monetarist; he claims to have compiled the first set of British money supply statistics at Birmingham University in the early 1960s. Walters was a signatory to 'Memorial to the Prime Minister' and wrote stockbrokers' circulars which attracted the attention of Sir Keith Joseph.

To take the ideas metaphor further: from flowing down mountain streams to being carried by breezes and then stronger forces, monetarist ideas in Britain by 1973 had acquired an almost gale-force intensity for their followers. There was nothing mysterious or conspiratorial about the way the various followers interacted. For example Brittan and Jay were naturally attracted to the work of those British academic monetarists who were, as it were, redefining the Chicago message for British consumption. A number of Tory MPs did their best to stir up interest in the subject. And when the Commons expenditure sub-committee embarked in the summer of 1974 on an examination of the relationship between public expenditure, inflation and the balance of payments, Professor Walters was chosen as the committee's specialist adviser, and Laidler was called as witness. Moreover, Laidler achieved something of a triumph by predicting that the monetary expansion of over 20 per cent per annum between 1971 and mid 1973 portended inflation of over 20 per cent by 1975; he also managed to predict a bigger recession than most experts were forecasting at the time, on the grounds that monetary policy, having previously been too lax, had recently become too tight.

'The Hi-jacking of a Political Party'

Let us take the position in the summer of 1974. Monetarism was still very much a minority cult, but because Jay and Brittan were in such important posts in the press, it was receiving publicity and approval out of all proportion to its standing in the economics profession and in the Bank of England and Whitehall (although the cult certainly had a few sympathizers there). Even while Laidler was making his predictions to the expenditure sub-committee, plenty of other witnesses were dismissing monetarism out of hand. Friedman had been accepted by British commentators, although he was still a highly controversial figure within the profession. There were many economists on both sides of the Atlantic who argued, for instance, that there might well be an association between inflation and money supply growth – in a way it was almost tautologous to say that monetary growth in excess of the growth of productivity was inflationary. The key question was: what is the direction of causality? Is inflation really caused by monetary growth, or is monetary growth the expression of underlying inflationary forces, principally costs, of which wages are the key element? Most economists took the latter view, and that was built up into the models they used to work out what was happening to the economy and what was likely to happen (the forecasts). The money supply was not even taken into account in the Treasury model in 1974, and only marginally in, for example, the London Business School model.

The most important convert to monetarism in 1974 was Sir Keith Joseph. After the fall of the Heath government, in which he had been Secretary for Health and Social Security, Sir Keith undertook an agonized reappraisal of policy. 'I reinvigorated old relationships which the barbarism of government tends to injure,' he recalled in 1982. 'I found Alan Walters very bitter – why had one put one's nose down at the DHSS and *allowed* such things to happen? We had seen the rate of inflation climbing fast, as Alan Walters had predicted in 1972; but I hadn't identified the key battle and fought it in government – not at all.' Sir Keith remembered being impressed in 1974 not only by what Walters told him, but also by Alfred Sherman – subsequently to become director of his Centre for Policy Studies – and Peter Bauer of the London School of Economics.* 'I resolved never again to get passionately involved in departmental concerns – however important – and miss the big issues.'

Apart from what he called 'the cycle of deprivation' in social policy, Sir Keith identified inflation and 'the erosion of the private enterprise dynamic' as the key issues.

I decided to devote myself to trying to persuade anyone interested that Western European countries had done better for their peoples, whatever the names of the governing parties, by using the engine of a decentralized, profit-seeking competitive economic system more understandingly than we had done. I decided to promote what I called 'continence' – an effort to get back to less deficits, because I understood from the Alan Walters and Peter Bauers of this world that deficit financing and borrowing were one of the main causes of our troubles, though they in turn were the result of other problems – management, the unions, incompetence . . .[3]

What happened after this was 'constructive reappraisal' in the eyes of what for a short time became the Joseph camp, and blatant treachery in the eyes of the Heath men. Joseph was nominally the opposition spokesman on home affairs in 1974, but he devoted more and more of his time to economic matters. Both Joseph and the Heath men agree that Joseph went to Heath and asked his permission to found the CPS so that he could explore how private enterprise and social market policies worked in other countries, particularly Germany, and how Britain might learn the lessons. After that, accounts and interpretations differ.

Sir Keith became the founder and chairman of the CPS. The president was Margaret Thatcher. The full-time director – a man who was to have greater access to Mrs Thatcher at No. 10 Downing Street than the average man from a research institute – was Mr Alfred Sherman, who had started life on the extreme left, ultimately seen what he regarded as the light on the extreme right, and became a frequent contributor to the *Daily Telegraph*. Sherman, the editor of the various policy studies subsequently published by the CPS, got

* Well known for his belief in the corrupting influences of welfare payments and overseas aid.

straight to the point in his prefaces: 'Our object is to reshape the climate of opinion. The Centre proposes to fight vigorously on this front of the battle of ideas.' (He was knighted in 1983.)

To this day Mr Heath's closest associates feel bitter about the way the CPS was set up. Said one:

It was a fraud. Keith Joseph went to Ted and asked his permission to set up a fund to see how private enterprise worked in other countries. Then he went round the City saying he had Heath's permission to raise money. Then it became the Joseph /Thatcher power base for attacking everything Ted stood for.

Heath put nominees on the CPS board: Robert Carr, his former Secretary for Employment, and Adam Ridley, who had gone from the Department of Economic Affairs in the 1960s to the Heath Think Tank under Lord Rothschild, and subsequently to the Conservative research department.

The key alliance, however, was that of Sir Keith Joseph and Margaret Thatcher, urged on by Sherman. Mrs Thatcher's biographers speak of her basic political instincts being formed very early – 1945 rather than 1974–75. However, there is precious little evidence of any monetarist flirtations on her part before 1974: she was a busy departmental minister who kept out of – and was kept out of – economic policy under the Heath administration. Her right-wing instincts, and her Grantham grocer's daughter's approach to household economics, may have made her a willing recipient from Keith Joseph of the monetarist ideas he was so enthusiastically expounding during 1974. But it has to be said that, before the prospect of the leadership arose, such ideas were conspicuous only by their absence. Indeed, Sir Keith and Mrs Thatcher had been the 'big spenders' of the Heath administration.

Whatever the purity of Sir Keith's original intentions, the CPS and the course taken by Sir Keith soon began to give the Heath men strong grounds for suspicion. It did not take long for the study of other European economies to give way to the propagation of anti-Heath views.

These were at first kept within the CPS and the Shadow

Cabinet. But Joseph failed to persuade either Robert Carr, under the auspices of the CPS, or the Shadow Cabinet itself. He then brought his views out into the open in a major speech at Preston Town Hall which was to prove the harbinger of a turning point in post-war British economic policy. The speech caused a furore inside and outside the Shadow Cabinet. Edward Heath never forgave Joseph for breaking ranks – nor for the manner in which he chose to do so. Sir Keith explained the matter to me thus:

I only made the speech at Preston after failing to persuade the Shadow Cabinet. My speech involved a critique of what we had done in 1970–74 which I saw as constructive in motivation. I did not want to be a rival to Edward Heath. I had tried to convert him and failed.[4]

Sir Keith Joseph made his move after much heated debate within the Shadow Cabinet, and much private agonizing outside it. He took exhaustive trouble over his first speech – commentators such as Samuel Brittan were among those who saw drafts and contributed ideas – trouble both in writing it and debating with himself over whether he should actually deliver it. The speech was on the subject of inflation. The message was monetarist – but not just monetarist: Sir Keith was many times to emphasize that 'Monetarism is not enough.' What it was crucially concerned with was unemployment, and Sir Keith went further than any mainstream British politician had done in admitting that governments did choose between inflation and unemployment, and came close to advocating an increase in unemployment in order to cure the 'greater evil' of inflation.

Many Tories have subsequently referred to the speech as being politically inept. Inept it may have been, but it was carefully thought out, and many people were consulted as to whether a public pronouncement which appeared to advocate higher unemployment in the short term (in order, it would argue, to reduce inflation, save society and benefit employment in the longer run) should be delivered at all. (I myself was consulted indirectly, by somebody close to Sir Keith: 'A major politician is thinking of risking his reputation making a speech which will appear to advocate higher unemployment. Should he do it?' 'No,' I said, without much difficulty.)

I mention this simply to show that Sir Keith certainly knew what he was doing, or what he was risking. He went ahead with the speech, delivered at Preston Town Hall on Wednesday 4 September 1974. It was a double political bombshell. With Labour in effect presiding over a hung Parliament, everybody was expecting another – the 'real' – general election in the autumn. The Conservative Party was still under the leadership of Edward Heath. Sir Keith was, quite apart from anything else, deliberately and publicly dissociating himself from the economics of the Heath administration – that was one bombshell. But he was also risking, in country and Parliament, his reputation as a humanitarian politician. For his argument that this was the humanitarian way in the long run was open, as we shall see, to a number of questions, even among the 'thinking' public who might be expected to read his speech – which was reproduced in full in the centre spread of a sympathetic *Times* two days later. The electorate at large, and perhaps the average back-bench MP, would certainly not be expected to wade through the subtleties of his analysis, let alone understand it. For them the message was 'Sir Keith advocates higher unemployment.' And since Sir Keith was saying that full employment should no longer be the foremost economic priority, this was a fair inference.

There were several strands in Sir Keith's analysis. He began with an apocalyptic warning that inflation was threatening to destroy British society and pave the way for dictatorship, at the same time accepting his full share of the collective responsibility of the governments that had allowed inflation to get a grip. He gave the impression of a sudden conversion by saying: 'I once believed that much of our inflation, *particularly recently* [my italics], was a product of rocketing world prices . . .' Now he knew it was 'the result of the creation of new money – and the consequent deficit financing – out of proportion to the additional goods and services available. When the money supply grows too quickly, inflation results.' He went on, 'it has always been known that to create too much money – "excess aggregate demand" is what the economists call it – is to court the danger of inflation.' Governments took the risks, because they worried about social tensions caused by unemployment. 'Experience has shown that far more menacing tensions are generated by inflation itself, and that, in circumstances of excess demand, they cannot be cured by incomes policy.'

Sir Keith chose his words about incomes policies carefully: 'I now see that any effective incomes policy must be based on sustaining the overall balance between demand and supply . . . if supply and demand are not in balance, if money is being pumped into the economy at a faster rate than the growth of goods and services, no incomes policy can conceivably mitigate inflation, let alone prevent it.' But then Sir Keith went on to give *The Times*, at least, the impression that he endorsed the findings of the expenditure sub-committee that had called Laidler as witness and employed Walters as special adviser, 'that incomes policy as such is neither desirable nor workable'.

Sir Keith then proceeded to make the fair but politically difficult point that, in essence, 'the unemployment figures do not mean what they say' – only when certain figures, or reasonable estimates, are deducted from the unemployment total (those on the register, but in the process of changing jobs; the unenthusiastic; the unemployable; the fraudulent; the elderly who are obliged to register in order to qualify for the retirement pension) 'do we have the real involuntary unemployed in the Keynesian sense, that is to say people who are both willing and able to work and who have been unemployed for over eight weeks. During the post-war period their numbers will have fluctuated between one and three hundred thousand or so.' After taking vacancies into account, Sir Keith went on: 'for almost the whole of the post-war period there were on a national basis several times as many real vacancies as involuntary unemployed, to use Keynes's term.' (Although regional disparities, he conceded, produced genuine unemployment in specific areas, which was why governments had specific regional policies.)

Mistaking the true levels of unemployment, Sir Keith went on to argue, governments had indulged in successive bouts of monetary expansion, which reduced unemployment for a time, but inevitably led to a 'stop' when the balance of payments ran into trouble. Inflation had meanwhile accelerated, but wages and prices alike were 'much more sticky in the face of downward pressures than when market pressures are pushing them upwards'. So the next burst of monetary creation, in response to rising unemployment during the stop, meant that inflation was accelerating from a higher starting point, and so on.

From criticizing excessive monetary growth in situations where demand exceeds supply, Joseph took the argument a stage further: successive governments had, on *several* occasions since the war [my italics], been faced with rising unemployment, but with home demand still in excess of supply, the balance of payments in deficit, and job vacancies well in excess of involuntarily unemployed. Sir Keith went on:

On each occasion, the government – by which I mean *almost every post-war government* – has chosen to boost home demand by deficit financing, in spite of the virtual certainty that the additional balance of payments deficits generated would oblige them to call a halt fairly soon and thereby lose at least as many jobs as they were creating, while keeping the additional inflation . . .

On such occasions, governments should weigh the short-lived benefits of up to four hundred thousand unemployed and their families against the permanent – and I repeat permanent – repercussions of such deficit financing on the whole population of 55 million people . . . the condition of 55 million people is even more important. We cannot talk about fighting inflation as the overriding priority and then in the same or another speech say that we can take no monetary action which might threaten some jobs. We cannot have it both ways.

The speech seemed to progress from the 'some' or 'several' occasions when governments had produced excess demand – a view from which few Keynesians would have dissented in retrospect – to a more general attack on deficit financing *per se*. Thus: 'What I am saying is that it is the methods that successive governments have used to reduce unemployment – namely expanding aggregate demand by deficit financing – which has created inflation, and without really helping the unemployed either.'

(Joseph then went to more immediately topical points – such as the way the new Labour administration had taken action to hurt the already suffering company sector. He urged Labour to drop its vendetta against business – which it was duly forced to do with emergency tax relief measures.)

The main proposal in the speech was a call for a three- or four-year 'gradualist' programme for phasing out excess demand in the economy and moving towards a non-inflationary growth for the money supply. 'If we get the money supply wrong – too high or too low – nothing will come right. Monetary control is a pre-essential for everything else we need and want to do.'

Reporting on the speech, Richard Evans, the *Financial Times* lobby correspondent, said:

There will be speculation that Sir Keith, in dissociating himself from the former Conservative administration's incomes policy and from reflation through the growth of money supply, is taking a calculated risk that the Tories will lose the coming election. He would then be in a strong position to lead the economic Right of the Tory Party which would gain ground in influence. He would also be able to attract the significant section of the party which is totally dissatisfied with present policies.

However sincere Sir Keith may have been in his views, his speech was sensationally disloyal to his leader. Even *The Times* itself, in a leading article that was fulsome in its praise for the speech, had to concede: 'By the standards of post-war politics Sir Keith Joseph has handed a blunderbuss loaded with duck shot to Mr Wilson and invited him to blow the Conservative Party's head off.'

The speech had many ironic consequences and implications. It was legitimately seen as a bid for the Tory leadership – but by a man who, by common consent of those closest to him, was given to inordinate self-doubt and agonizing bouts of indecision. He had set himself up as a potential leader, and gathered acolytes around him. But the same question applied to Joseph as to others who failed to get it eventually – such as a man with very different economic views, R. A. Butler: did he really want the leadership? And, if so, did he want it as much as leaders have to want it? And although his speech brought Joseph out in the open for a few months as leader of the Tory right – without the kind of associations with other views, such as on race, that the monetarist Enoch Powell was tainted with – it also frightened away not only the sort of MP with economic views that Mrs Thatcher was subsequently to dub 'wet' but also those who questioned his judgement in the remarks about unemployment, and the general disloyalty to his leader. (Joseph was not even Shadow Chancellor; he was Shadow Home Secretary.) The general election took place five weeks later, on 10 October; and the Tories lost.

The Joseph speech induced immediate rearguard action from Edward Heath and the Shadow Employment Secretary, James Prior. Heath insisted that counter-inflationary policies must be broadly based, and include incomes policy – preferably voluntary. He acknowledged that firm and consistent control over the money supply should be part of the broader economic policy package – not the 'pre-essential' standing Joseph had given it – and agreed that Conservatives 'may have lessons to learn from our past experience'. Prior, too, was prepared to acknowledge that mistakes had been made, but not to go overboard in the opposite direction. 'Our experience is that we got quite good control over incomes but we didn't get the demand factor right and we have to learn from that, and I am quite prepared to listen to Sir Keith and to go along with his views when he says we ought to learn from our past mistakes.'

The import of those moderate remarks by Heath and Prior was to be ignored by those who captured control of the Conservative economic policy. The more one studies the experience of the Heath administration and the Thatcher years, the more one is struck by the recurring theme of over-reaction, lack of proportion, and excessive swings of the pendulum of analysis and opinion.

Heath's 1970–74 administration had started with that fatal disavowal of incomes policies of any sort, and – whatever Sir Keith Joseph subsequently maintained – had seen unemployment rise to a level where at least one police chief was concerned about the threat to social order. The circumstances surrounding the rescue of Upper Clyde were an important factor in the wider U-turn in macro economic policy. But he over-reacted. Never had economic policy in Britain been so wildly expansionary as in 1972–73. Demand management *had* got out of hand. Was the right response to learn from this mistake, and try harder with the tools at the government's disposal – fiscal policy, monetary policy, exchange rate policy, incomes policy – or to abandon all faith in demand management and opt for a new religion? (We have seen that an influential minority of economists was flirting with monetarism before Mr Heath's U-turn. It was the economic experience of 1972–74 which cemented the relationship.) Whatever the monetarists who proved such a critical influence on Sir Keith Joseph may have thought about the timing of their own conversion, it took the excessive expansion of 1972–73 to put people like Sir Keith in a mood to be receptive to them. A crisis in the system whereby monetary policy was considered part of a total package (the weapons of economic management) – a crisis brought about partly because monetary policy was badly mishandled – led people to conclude that only monetary policy mattered. For, as we shall see, Sir Keith's subsequent assertion that 'Monetarism is not enough' did not imply acceptance of demand management. The strands of his thinking in economic policy were very much those of the monetarist academics and journalists referred to above – loss of faith in demand management and eager espousal of a creed which simultaneously offered a solution to inflation and said that demand management policies led to inflation and were futile anyway.

Sir Keith had not given voice on the evils of demand management *before* the 1972–73 episode. He had lived politically with such policies for twenty years or so. In his speech he seemed to project his horror at the events of 1972–73 progressively on to nearly all post-war governments' efforts at expansion – at much lower rates of inflation. He was speaking at a time when inflation was accelerating to what turned out to be the worst rate in recent history, when many people were indeed frightened. Nothing like such fright and moral indignation had been manifested during the previous twenty years of demand management policies aimed at what Sir Keith now regarded as having been 'overfull employment'. But all these years were brought into the evidence for the apocalyptic analysis.

In view of the influence the 1972–73 period had on Sir Keith Joseph and Margaret Thatcher, and in view of the influence they had on economic policy from 1979 onwards, it is worth exploring the factors which went wrong in that first period, and asking whether the abandonment of demand management and the espousal of monetarism were sensible reactions.

Whatever the rights and wrongs of the argument about monetarism, there can be little question that during the Heath Mark Two period – indeed, from the summer of 1971 onwards – monetary policy was lax. So – eventually – was fiscal policy. So was exchange rate policy.

It did not need the money supply figures to demonstrate this laxity. That good old Keynesian budget deficit was being expanded fast. It was not so much a case of demand management not working, as of demand management working excessively well. Unemployment was brought down, and rapid economic growth was achieved over a period of two years. Expansion of public spending was inaugurated in the autumn of 1971, and there were two expansionary Budgets in 1972. When the pound and the balance of payments ran into trouble in the summer of 1972, the pound was allowed to float down, so as not to be a constraint on expansion. Nothing was to impede the dash for growth. And monetary policy became vigorously supportive of growth. In this a change in the methods of monetary management exerted an important influence.

For some years the Bank of England had wanted to increase competition in the banking system. It was argued that the system of quantitative control over bank advances restricted competition and innovation. And it accorded with the 'market' philosophy of the Heath Mark One administration that people should be able to obtain bank loans if they needed them, provided they paid the market price. Quantitative controls were therefore abandoned with the introduction of the new policy of Competition and Credit Control (CCC) in April 1971. But the 'rationing by price' policy soon became one of loans for all: as part of the dash for growth, Heath urged lower interest rates in the effort to persuade industrialists to invest in new plant and machinery. And under Chancellor Tony Barber's tax reforms, bank loans were made tax-deductible for almost all purposes – including the purchase of homes, second homes and shares. These latter innovations were certainly consistent with the Conservative 'property-owning democracy' slogan going back to Anthony Eden's day. But they encouraged the biggest credit binge in British post-war economic history.

The subsequent share and property price boom has spawned a reading list in itself; and the consequences of the eventual bursting of the bubble are still a regular topic of discussion in the City of London. In theory, under CCC the Bank of England was controlling the money supply; in practice it argued that the change in the system was making the figures – money supply grew at over 20 per cent per annum between summer 1971 and summer 1973 – difficult to interpret.

One of the ironies of this episode – and indeed of the whole monetarist saga – is that in the fifties and sixties, the period when Sir Keith thought things were so lax, there had been long periods of tight monetary control. Attention had been focused not literally on the money supply – the deposit side of the banking system's balance sheets – but on the figures on the right-hand side of the accounts: bank advances. Such rationing by credit controls may have offended market purists, but it did allow the Treasury and the Bank of England to control the growth of bank advances more effectively than, as it turned out, they controlled the money supply in 1971–73.

To a large extent, however, monetary policy played a

subsidiary role during the long period of fixed exchange rates which ended, for the pound, in June 1972. This was largely because monetary policy under the pre-1972 fixed exchange rate system was subsumed by exchange rate policy. If the pound was under pressure because of balance of payments trouble – which monetary economists would argue was a sign of lax monetary policy – then the Bank Rate would be raised with a view to restoring balance.

When the pound was floated in 1972, monetary policy was no longer being determined by the automatic pilot of the fixed exchange rate, and therefore became more important, relative to fiscal policy, in the scheme of things. But as we have seen, under CCC monetary policy was simply let loose. It was undoubtedly stimulating aggregate demand, raising the prices of assets – a stock exchange boom; a boom in house prices – making people richer, more willing to spend, and all in an atmosphere of easy, tax-deductible credit.

Thus although monetary policy theoretically assumed greater importance under floating exchange rates, it was in one sense abandoned. Inflation was almost actively courted: it was not going to be allowed to stand in the way of economic growth. So that if there was an exchange rate crisis – signifying, perhaps, too lax a monetary policy – the response was not to be higher interest rates to protect the balance of payments. The exchange rate was, in the words of officials of the time, 'to take the strain'. And if the strain was taken, this was to lead, via higher import prices, to a higher inflation rate.

Economic policy during 1972–73 shifted from one extreme to the other and then stayed there. By any standard there was excess demand pushing prices up. But there was also a strong cost push element, resulting from tougher union bargaining in the 1970s than in the 1960s, and from the (unfortunately timed) 'threshold agreement' system, under which, in the latter phases of the Heath incomes policy, wages were automatically allowed to rise to reflect the cost of living increases. Since this period coincided with the boost to import prices caused by first a near doubling of commodity prices and then the oil price explosion of

1973–74, the threshold system could hardly have been worse timed. And while Sir Keith was preparing his speeches, the Labour administration – which wanted first to win the election of October 1974 and then to have a successful outcome to the EEC referendum of summer 1975 – was determined to do nothing to upset the unions on the wages front.

I have argued elsewhere[5] that there was a quantum leap in the influence of the unions in wage bargaining between the sixties and the early seventies. This was attributable partly to their reaction against the successive – but not successful – attempts by Labour and Tories to rein them in to that no man's land of tougher legislation. It was also affected by governmental reaction to the unions' reaction: having failed, as it were, to beat them, governments actively courted the unions and invited them in on some of their economic discussions. This coincided with greater union awareness of the effect that the inflation to which their wage claims contributed was having on their real gains. They wanted to be compensated for past inflation, even to anticipate future inflation. As the monetarists pointed out, this helped to explain why there was less of a 'trade-off' between unemployment and inflation, and both could rise simultaneously. They argued that there was a kind of ratchet effect, moving wage inflation higher. The apotheosis of union awareness and governmental desire to please was seen in the threshold agreement system, which goes a long way to explaining why inflation rose so high in this period.

In asking for tolerance of higher unemployment, Sir Keith was in effect wanting to restore the trade-off between unemployment and inflation (known by economists as the Phillips Curve, after A. W. Phillips, who had pointed to an inverse relationship between the growth of money wages and unemployment in a seminal article in Economica in 1958).

As if these were not enough factors tending towards excess demand and more inflationary pressures in the economy, there was the basic background influence of a more inflationary world picture. Many economists have traced the accelerating world inflation to the Vietnam war, and the US government's failure to finance it in a non-inflationary way. The 1960s were boom times for the US anyway, and the Vietnam war added considerable inflationary pressure. So, just as the Heath dash for growth was a clear case of Keynesian policies being abused, overdone and causing an acceleration in inflation, so the background of accelerating world inflation can be attributed not to Keynesianism per se, but to its abuse in the US.

The Vietnam factor was evident in the late 1960s. It was augmented by the fact that in the early seventies there were almost synchronized attempts at expansion by many of the leading industrial countries, which put pressure on commodity prices, notably oil, and fuelled world inflation.

In sum, therefore, there was an acceleration in world inflation, but a particularly strong British component on top. In a survey of British inflationary experience since the war, Professor Arthur Brown of Leeds University found little evidence of monetary laxity causing inflation – as opposed to cost push from union wage demands being 'financed' by the Central Bank. But he did find such evidence in 1971–73.[6]

By any standards the experience of 1971–73 was exceptional, although nonetheless disturbing for that. But it led Sir Keith Joseph and his followers to leap from the conclusion that lax monetary policy contributed to a dangerous inflation in the early 1970s to the conclusion that lax monetary policy was the main cause of the inflation of the early 1970s; this then led them to the conclusion that lax monetary policies had caused earlier inflations, and thence to the conclusion that Keynesian policies of demand management had been a disaster since their inception and that monetary control – begging the question of how this was to be achieved – was the answer to the problem of inflation. And urging them on in all this were the monetarists who claimed to have discovered the magic solution and the need for it even before the experience which initially so disturbed Sir Keith.

The Centre for Policy Studies, with offices in Wilfred Street, Westminster, was to be the base for publishing a whole series of books and pamphlets devoted to the monetarist and right-wing cause from 1974 onwards. Among other things, it published the speeches of Thatcher and Joseph, works such as 'Second Thoughts on Full Employment Policy' by Samuel Brittan, and 'Myths and Magic in Economic Management' by Jock Bruce-Gardyne (who lost his parliamentary seat in 1974 and was a consultant to the CPS from October 1974).

The CPS became the formal political manifestation of the ideology which had so far been propagated by the nominally independent Institute for Economic Affairs. Both were in the propaganda business. Both had offices in relatively unassuming private houses in S.W.1. Both poured out a stream of publications designed partly to reassure the faithful but first and foremost to proselytize. And both were in close contact with the principal political and economic figures in our story of the rise of economic evangelicalism.

If there was a division of labour between the two institutions, it was the concentration of the CPS on the universities – Sir Keith himself was to embark on a series of lectures around the country – and of the older institution, the IEA, on Fleet Street and the City. The IEA, for instance, holds regular monthly lunches at which the faithful mingle with City and Fleet Street.

As we have seen, by the time of Joseph's seminal Preston speech, the evangelical bridgeheads were well established; further strong advances were to be made in the next few years. The features, leading articles and political columns of the *Daily Telegraph* and *Daily Mail* were easy converts to the new religion. In addition to Samuel Brittan on the *Financial Times* and Peter Jay on *The Times*, monetarism also won over *The Times*'s editor, William Rees-Mogg; and monetarism and the IEA/CPS approach to life received strong support from Ronald Butt, who wrote on politics regularly for *The Times* and the *Sunday Times*. Even the *Guardian* for a time gave free vent to monetarism through the pen of Hamish McRae, its financial editor. Such converts were to prove valuable constituents of the new movement's power base in the next few years.

The conversions of people like Sir Keith seem to have been after the manner of a sudden vision on the road to Damascus.

The wide climate of opinion changed more slowly, however: it was after the shambles created by the economic policies of Labour in 1974–76 that monetarism showed signs of gaining its first foothold in practical policy-making. In particular, I am struck by the virtual unanimity of the people I have talked to on the question of Heath's downfall: monetarism or new ideology was not the major issue in the 1975 Tory leadership election.

But Heath's downfall is certainly a vivid landmark in the rise of monetarism and the move of the Tory balance of power to the right. We have seen that Heath flirted with right-wing and deflationary policies in 1970–71; and that many of his subsequent troubles arose because he reacted too violently in the opposite direction. This over-reaction was acknowledged by both Heath and Prior in their remarks after Joseph's Preston speech. From everything that is known about Edward Heath – and particularly from his economic thinking as seen in his speeches since 1975 – there is precious little evidence, or ground for suspicion, that had Heath remained leader, he would have wanted to move significantly to the right.

Clearly, the existence of a more prominent right-wing faction would have exerted pressure on Heath – and possibly had some influence, just as monetarism was to have some impact on Labour's policies in the middle phase of Denis Healey's Chancellorship. But what happened contemporaneously with Heath's downfall was that the Tory leadership came into the hands of someone who *wanted* to move the party to the right.

That someone was not Keith Joseph, but Margaret Thatcher. It is tempting to get carried away by the machinations of the Tory leadership election. But from the point of view of this book the key point is that, in several senses, it did not matter whether the leadership fell into the hands of Joseph or Thatcher: from the viewpoint of the rise of economic evangelicalism, it was vital that one of them should get it. They were the power base for monetarism in the Shadow Cabinet; Joseph was – until the events which led him to withdraw from the leadership contest – the more senior candidate. (As it turned out, it took some time, when she did come forward, for the world to take Margaret Thatcher's candidature seriously.) Joseph was Mrs Thatcher's mentor: she would certainly not, she told many at the time, have stood against 'Keith'.

The general tenor of the bitter Shadow Cabinet debates preceding the declaration of war at Preston was, in the words of one participant, 'for Joseph to attack Heath-type policies, Peter Walker to defend them, Mrs Thatcher to say "I agree with Keith", Geoffrey Howe to see something in what both sides said, and Ted to sum up with vehement criticism of whatever Joseph was propagating at the time.'

Preston was both the public marker for the rise of monetarism in the party and the first sign of the dawning realization that, quite apart from his opinions, Sir Keith's political judgement was faulty. Paradoxically it sowed the first seeds of doubt in people's minds about Sir Keith's qualifications for leading the party, while sparking off a series of unpredictable events which were to end up ensuring that the ideology represented by the Preston speech – and the faulty judgement – would triumph; but in the person of Margaret Thatcher.

The second episode which was to discredit Sir Keith's political judgement seriously in the minds of his fellow MPs was a speech in which he appeared to advocate differential contraception on a class basis. This prompted the private comment from one of his opponents: 'First he wants to make the workers unemployed; now he wants to castrate them.'

Meanwhile, back in the jungle, as it were, the Tories had lost the second general election in 1974 on 10 October. Back-benchers, in the shape of the executive of the 1922 Committee, were out for Heath's blood, and the Heath supporters felt, among other things, that Sir Keith's Preston speech had hardly helped Edward Heath's chances in the election. He was now being blamed for having lost.

Wilson now had an overall majority. Heath was seen as having been unforgivably careless in losing not one or two but three elections. He had been the first beneficiary of the Tories' conversion from the 'customary processes of consultation' for selecting leaders to formal election within the parliamentary party. He was to become the first victim of the party's new internal democratic process and to suffer the double humiliation of being rejected by country and party.

The removal of Heath was a long-drawn-out affair – 'a bit like a bull-fight' in the words of one observer at the time. The Shadow Cabinet, with certain obvious exceptions, was in favour of his staying; so, when consulted, was the party at large. It was the back-benchers who went for him – and they were the ones with the votes.

In retrospect this important link in the rise of monetarism had, to the outsider, some notably unjust elements. Two of the elections Heath lost – those in March 1966 and October 1974 – were really one half of an election: there was a hung Parliament, and the Labour leader – in each case Wilson – was going to the country, at a time of his own choosing, to finish off the job. Moreover Heath's victory in the June 1970 general election was largely unexpected, and very much his own triumph.

In so far as it was a policy vote, the parliamentary party's vote against Heath was essentially against the ignominious manner in which he had staked all and lost in the February 1974 election, precipitated by the miners' strike, on the issue of 'Who governs?' Clearly, the small right-wing and monetarist clique now wanted Heath to be removed on policy grounds. But to effect this they needed – given the right, left and centre composition of the parliamentary party – the support of many who were not fundamentally opposed to Heath on his general strategy, but who clearly hoped he had learned something from his unfortunate tactical handling of the February election.

The Gadarene rush of back-bench MPs away from Heath in the leadership election of early 1975 is explicable only in terms of a personal vote against Heath – the pack chanting 'Ted must go', with little thought of the morrow, and of who was to replace him. It is in this light that comments such as 'Ted went, and then came monetarism' begin to make sense. The evidence for the personal feelings against Heath, and for the view that power had adulterated the former Chief Whip's relations with his own parliamentary colleagues, is available *passim* in Sir Nigel Fisher's book. The moral for party leaders is clear.

The role of the 1922 Committee executive – the inner circle of Tory back-benchers – in all this will no doubt be clarified in memoirs to come. Fisher, a member of the Committee at the time and not a right-winger, is scrupulously fair to Edward du Cann, who as chairman of the 1922 Committee, a possible leader, and a man who was deposed seven years earlier by Heath as chairman of the party, was alleged by some to have gone beyond the customary impartiality of chairmanship in the campaign to remove Heath.

The principal evidence against Heath advanced by the 1922 executive was said to emanate 'from the doorsteps' – not the party at large, which on the whole made a loyal response when sounded out (voteless though it was over the leadership). At all events Heath was forced into conceding what in effect was a vote of confidence, and he lost. Willie Whitelaw, who would almost certainly have beaten Mrs Thatcher in the first ballot, refused to stand against his leader. But by the time he did stand in the second ballot (Heath had withdrawn after the first), Mrs Thatcher's bandwagon was well and truly rolling.

Mrs Thatcher had assumed Sir Keith Joseph's mantle when he stood down after an agonized personal appraisal of his own political judgement and suitability. There had then been a question whether Mrs Thatcher would stand against Edward du Cann, but the latter decided not to try for the leadership – he had troubles on his hands at the City bank Keyser Ullmann, where he was chairman, and there was the prospect of adverse press publicity on Keyser Ullmann's affairs. Having inherited Keith Joseph's supporters, Mrs Thatcher then gained many of du Cann's. She had got her power base, and her chief lieutenant, the late Airey Neave, did some highly effective campaigning among the old and new members of the parliamentary party who hardly knew Mrs Thatcher personally. Neave's campaign is variously described as 'brilliant' by Thatcher supporters and 'below the belt' by many of the Whitelaw supporters. And, as luck would have it, Heath – greatly underrating Mrs Thatcher as a threat – had chosen her to fight the Finance Bill in the Commons, which she did to the considerable admiration of many of her colleagues, as number two to the then Shadow Chancellor, Robert Carr.

Mrs Thatcher, then, who was to oversee the rise of economic evangelicalism to a position of considerable power, was a rank outsider, 'an accident' in the view of many Tory MPs. In a sense she was that stereotype for which there are many precedents in the history of the Tory leadership – the compromise candidate. The difference is that she was an extremist compromise candidate. But, once Joseph had dropped out, her candidacy was indispensable to the economic evangelicals' cause.

REFERENCES

1. *Britain's Economic Problem* (1976).
2. 'Second Thoughts on Full Employment Policy' (1975).
3. Interview with the author, 8 June 1982.
4. ibid.
5. *Who Runs the Economy?* (1979).
6. British Academy lecture, May 1980.

CHAPTER THREE

THE TORIES IN OPPOSITION, 1975–79

Monetarism and Economic Evangelicalism
gain a Bridgehead in Britain

To people who consider themselves the natural party of government the role of opposition does not come naturally. It is part of the received wisdom of British political analysis that Labour is a natural party of opposition, but that the Conservatives are decidedly uneasy in that role, and do not quite know what to make of it.

As with so much received wisdom, there is a liberal sprinkling of mythology in the assumption. One has only to think of the typical Labour administration, coming into office with a heavy coating of left-wing manifesto commitments, to realize that there is a fair amount of opposition for any Tory government to undertake. Between 1945 and 1979, moreover, periods of opposition were almost equally divided between Conservative and Labour.

It will be recalled from the last chapter that Mrs Thatcher herself had had a timely opportunity to show her talents for opposition during the Finance Bill debates of 1974 as number two to the Shadow Chancellor, Robert (now Lord) Carr. She seized her chance, and this rise to debating prominence stood her in good stead during the Tory leadership stakes. (There are some who would argue, from her performance then and since she has been in office as Prime Minister, that Mrs Thatcher is a natural one-woman opposition party in herself.)

By the time of the 1979 election the traditional Tory assumption about their divine right to office had been a little shaken. For one thing, the party had in fact been in office for only four of the previous fifteen years. For another, right from the time of the Home affair and the loss of the 1964 election, the party had demonstrated considerable unease about its

precise role in the modern world. The agonies over the
leadership were one reflection of this. The question whether,
after Heath's humiliating defeat at the hands of the miners,
the Tories could effect any sort of working relationship with
the trade unions was another. (Nobody had yet suggested
solving this problem by abolishing the unions.) For a time
there was a further serious matter for concern: the theory
that Labour, via its more natural relationship with these
overpowering unions, was itself perhaps the natural party of
British government in the modern world – a theory backed
by yet another: the suggestion that, as more and more sons
and daughters of the working class moved into the middle
class, demographic trends were themselves operating against
the Tories. Sociologists might call this the 'proletarianization
of the bourgeoisie'. On the other hand, we have seen that an
appreciable proportion of the 'working class' vote Conservative already. And it is a reasonable assumption that many
'upwardly mobile' people switch to the Tories anyway.

Whether Mrs Thatcher's selection as leader is considered
an accident, the workings of Providence, or a compromise,
there is nothing unusual in Tory history in unfancied
candidates suddenly coming up on the outside – or even, to
stick to the racing metaphor, on the rails. Nor is there
anything unusual (we can take the brief ascendancy of Lord
Home as an exception which proves the rule) in the Tories
choosing a leader who is 'right for the times', if not in
keeping with the most recently held assumption about the
ideal type of Tory leader. Disraeli was one such candidate;
Churchill is the outstanding example; Heath was thought to
be another.

Whatever the criticisms to be developed in this book about
her performance in government, Mrs Thatcher too was in
certain respects a product of the times. Experience in 1978–79
was to show that Labour did not, after all, possess a monopoly
of ability to handle the trade unions, and this point was not
to escape the notice of the electorate. Even later, after three
years during which unemployment doubled to over three
million, Mrs Thatcher's populist touch was to give her
ratings in the opinion polls that one might have been

reluctant to risk money on a year earlier. Admittedly this was to be after the Falklands affair, when her popularity could be said to have been based on the dying Henry IV's advice to Henry V: 'Busy giddy minds with foreign quarrels.'

Mrs Thatcher's period as opposition leader – February 1975 to May 1979 – was to give her good practice for the populism she was to rely on in power. It was also to administer a severe blow to the theory that the Conservatives do not know what to apply their minds to when in opposition.

Another popular political assumption about the Tories is that it is only relatively recently that they have given thought to the serious process of formulating policy while in opposition. It can equally be argued that during the years – especially pre-war – when they were in office most of the time, the question of policies in opposition did not arise; and since the war, during each period of opposition, the new blood has rewritten history and deluded itself into thinking 'Now, for the first time, we are making a serious effort to formulate policy.'

Thus a number of the people involved in the 1975–79 policy discussions talk as if there was little serious preparation in 1964–70. And the Heath men prided themselves during that period on doing more serious preparation than their predecessors. What, one wondered, would Lord Butler have made of that? Yet there are preparations and preparations: there is fuss and bother; there is the outward appearance of activity; and there is real change and progress, which may or may not arise as a result of the activity seen on the surface.

In several respects the opposition's programme is predetermined; and in one respect it is outside its control. Most of the jobs, and therefore the demands on the Shadow Cabinet's time, are taken up by the task of opposing: of reacting to events. One might go further: if, as many students of government believe, modern governmental activity consists largely of reacting to events, then the role of opposition is perhaps to react to people who are themselves reacting to events.

The second area in which the opposition's role is determined is in the natural order of the system by which a party is run. Within Parliament, the party is reacting to the government; in the country at large, it is reacting to itself. The early months and years of new-found opposition are years of inquest. Why did we lose? Where did we go wrong? What policies will stop us from losing the next election? Further: what policies will help us *win* the next election?

Given that the government has a reasonable working majority, there is little, in practice, that the opposition can do to stop it from doing more or less what it wants, at least in time of peace. The constraints on a government's economic policy can be many, but they seldom come from the other side of the floor – except (and this was to be important to the Tories in 1979) as an inheritance with which they are lumbered.

The most important outward sign of what a party does when out of office – apart from the day-to-day business of opposition in Westminster – is not so much the rewriting of history as the remaking of the manifesto. At one level, the thrust of their work can be seen as a labyrinthine committee process, in which they are drawing up the list of promises and commitments which they will undertake to honour during their next term of office. The manifesto-writing process is an important ritual, with many cans of midnight oil being burned to see that the phrases are right – at least to the satisfaction of those who feel the most passionately. The process is twofold. Much considered thought is given to the first, long-drawn-out stage, and much less to the second: hasty commitments are made which may well prove almost totally incompatible with the achievement of the more considered areas over which all that midnight oil was burned.

The annual party conference fits neatly – possibly to the embarrassment of the manifesto-drafters – into this policy-making pattern. The stirring speeches and the tribal cries of the Tory conference are the way the faithful and their leaders let off steam. Beneath the headlines and in the bars and corridors the important ritual proceeds by which the Shadow

Cabinet reports back to the activists from the constituencies and the latter pass on their messages and demands.

It is obvious to anybody who watches the Tory conference on television that the right wing is not the silent majority. But, as we have seen, there was more loyalty towards Heath when soundings were taken within the party organization than was emerging from the executive of the 1922 Committee. From 1975 onwards, however, there was to be no conflict between the basic instincts of the party activists and their new leader. Mrs Thatcher would be preaching to, and taking soundings from, the converted.

The twin themes of the early years of Mrs Thatcher's leadership were the purge by the right and the fight back by the left of the party. Heath men such as Michael Woolf were removed from Central Office, and old faithfuls instated or reinstated. In this regard it is interesting that Lord Thorneycroft, who had resigned from Mr Macmillan's administration on a monetarist principle in 1958, was made chairman of the party. Mrs Thatcher had, it is said by one of her biographers, long been an admirer of Lord Thorneycroft. (Yet Thorneycroft was subsequently to give the strong impression of being out of sympathy with Thatcherism when Mrs Thatcher finally came into office.)

One or two figures who had previously been thought of as Heath men suddenly changed their colour – or should one say were seen for the first time in their true colours? At all events, both Sir Geoffrey Howe and Mr Nigel Lawson – later Chancellor and Financial Secretary to the Treasury – became, with varying degrees of subtlety, more obviously identified with the monetarist camp. And David Howell did an abrupt about-turn. John Biffen, long a monetarist sympathizer, was closely involved in the leader's counsels. John Nott, as Shadow Trade Secretary, had also come to espouse the monetarist cause. Keith Joseph himself was now given overall responsibility for policy and research, and from March 1977 was also opposition spokesman on industry – a department he thought should be abolished. Sir Geoffrey Howe was made Shadow Chancellor.

While making changes at Central Office, Mrs Thatcher did

not have to alter the composition of the Shadow Cabinet much. What happened was the combination of a realignment of jobs, and the emergence of the monetarist wing in its true colours. Mrs Thatcher turned out to be more cautious – or deceptively cautious – than some of her detractors had expected. Tory heavyweights such as William Whitelaw, Lord Carrington and Francis Pym retained their places in the Shadow Cabinet (it is difficult to see how a Lady from Nowhere could suddenly have removed them). And there is even the lingering suggestion that Mrs Thatcher offered – or half offered – the possibility of a job to Edward Heath. (In the latter case it is equally difficult to understand how she could have done. At all events Heath is said to have refused it – and his supporters say he was never offered it.)

What was to be important from the economic policy point of view however – although not perhaps fully appreciated at the time – was that the economic roles fell at a very early stage into the hands of the monetarists, or those who were to prove susceptible to monetarism, whether intellectually or purely politically, with a view to their own personal advancement. It was quite a marked change for the party to move, in 1975, from a position where Edward Heath was leader, and Robert Carr (very much a moderate Heath man) Shadow Chancellor, to a point where Margaret Thatcher was leader, Sir Geoffrey Howe, Shadow Chancellor, and Sir Keith Joseph very close to the leader's ear on economic policy.

Before moving on to the role played by Sir Geoffrey in all this, we should emphasize one further point about Sir Keith. He and his Centre for Policy Studies had been the fulcrum for the lever which had removed Edward Heath. And although Sir Keith did not win the leadership himself, he was to play a very influential role in Mrs Thatcher's counsels. He had lost the personal battle against Heath – indeed he had withdrawn from the contest. But he had scored resounding gains in the policy war. And Mrs Thatcher, the beneficiary of his withdrawal from the race, was never to forget the debt she owed him.

The choice of Sir Geoffrey Howe as Shadow Chancellor was a fascinating one. Unlike Joseph, behind whose public hard line lay an agonized diffidence, Howe nearly always managed in public, in however low a key, and sometimes in the face of nerve-racking opposition, to radiate a sense of complacency. He saw himself, in his own words, as a 'Welsh fundamentalist'; he certainly did not give the impression in public of a man tortured by self-doubt. He had managed, in the years before 1975, to acquire a public reputation – and, for that matter, a private one among his colleagues – as a man who would be the last person to espouse monetarism. Through his speeches and his early articles in *Crossbow*, the periodical of the Tory Bow Group, Howe had given most people the impression he was well on the left of his party. Yet during his 1979–83 Chancellorship he was to maintain that his earlier writings were fully consistent with his subsequent position.

There are, of course, those who are left on some issues and right on others: indeed one convert to the monetarist cause to whom we have already referred, Samuel Brittan, once wrote a book called *Left or Right? The Bogus Dilemma*, and emphasized in his subsequent work that, although he now espoused monetarism, he was still 'left' – or what other people would call 'left' – on other issues.

This brings us to a definition and a distinction highly pertinent to this examination of the rise of monetarism, which will be explored further: 'economic liberalism'. Economic liberalism is that strand in the thinking of the Thatcher/Joseph school which derives from the old nineteenth-century Liberal tradition, in favour of free trade rather than protectionism, and laissez-faire rather than planning. Economic liberals tend to be anti-Keynesian, in that they laud the virtues of the unfettered market place, and vehemently oppose the kind of state activities which the Butskellite consensus took for granted – not least those designed to influence the level of output and employment in the economy through the management of demand.

Sir Geoffrey Howe expressed surprise to me in an interview 19 April 1982 that anybody should ever have thought of him as being 'left' in economic matters, and maintained that he had always been an economic liberal. Perhaps the misunderstanding arose because, unlike many of his fellow economic liberals and monetarists, Sir Geoffrey has, for many years, been a supporter of at least one manifestation of 'state encroachment': the Macmillan government's innovation of the National Economic Development Council, at which ministers, employers and unions sit round a table once a month to discuss economic and industrial issues. Sir Geoffrey has expressed the hope that around the NEDC table people could come to 'commonsense conclusions about the need to restrict pay demands to what the nation can afford, and to what is sensible from the point of view of effects of excessive wage settlements on employment'.

It was perhaps in this light that Sir Geoffrey, in turn, was seen by some – at least for a time – as a 'compromise candidate' as Shadow Chancellor: sympathetic to monetarism and the emergent economic liberals on the one hand; but with a commitment to at least part of the 'consensus' style approach to the economy that the heavyweights inherited by Mrs Thatcher would approve of, or be comforted by, even if they themselves were left out of the economic policy-making side, or not especially interested.

What deceived some of his Shadow Cabinet colleagues was Sir Geoffrey's apparently whole-hearted espousal of the Heath-style policies during the administration of 1970–74. Apart from anything else, Sir Geoffrey was, for a time, the Cabinet minister directly responsible for prices. But Howe says that it was that very experience which turned him away from incomes policies and what was being branded as the 'corporatist' approach to economic policy (of which more below: see page 78). Howe, and the then Chancellor Anthony Barber, were campaigning in the front line of prices and incomes policies with decreasing conviction; what turned Howe against the incomes policy approach that seemed consistent with the pro-Neddy side of his thinking, and towards the monetarism which did not sit easily with the Neddy approach, was the conclusion that the unions were, in that winter of 1973–74 and the miners' strike, 'not being reasonable'.

Howe's vision was of sensible men sitting round a table

discussing wage claims with an eye to the common good; what he encountered in the detailed administration of incomes policy was, as he saw it, groups of organized Labour with little respect for such procedures, who would use any excuse to try to add x per cent to their own particular settlement, as a 'special case'. The operation of a statutory incomes policy in practice did not accord with Howe's understanding of the rule of law. The attempt at building up a body of case law was not, he thought, being allowed to work. Special pleading was triumphant.

Given that, under Heath's incomes policy, there seemed to be scant respect for the law as he saw it, Geoffrey Howe found himself, like other Tories who were in the process of joining the monetarist camp, increasingly irritated by the bureaucratic nature of incomes policies, and it was this frustration, rather than the failure of the Heath Industrial Relations Act (which Sir Geoffrey had drafted), that drove him to examine the monetarist route – a route towards which the economic liberal in his make-up was already pointing.

It would have been out of keeping with the character of the man for Sir Geoffrey's conversion to have been as sudden an affair as Sir Keith Joseph's. There had been mild signs of it in the difficult setting of Edward Heath's ill-fated Shadow Cabinet of 1974. As Shadow Chancellor and chairman of the opposition's economic committee in the 1975–79 period, Howe was in a stronger position of influence than some observers at the time gave him credit for. He tended to be overshadowed on public occasions by Mrs Thatcher, who at one press conference during the election campaign was heard to say 'Don't just sit there, Geoffrey, say something.' Similarly, Howe's somewhat wooden performance in the Commons against Denis Healey – who once compared being attacked by Sir Geoffrey to 'being savaged by a dead sheep' – may have made outside observers underrate his influence and tenacity. The point about his disillusionment with incomes policy is that it provided an important link in the chain which was to drag monetarism to the centre of the Conservative stage. Woefully misconceived views about what monetarism, as they understood it, could achieve on

the inflation front were to play a major role in the errors of
policy during the early years of the Thatcher administration.

Nevertheless, it would be a mistake to jump from under-
stating Sir Geoffrey's influence to overstating it. Both in
opposition and in office Howe was considered by an over-
whelming majority of witnesses to be overshadowed, if not
dominated, by the personality and wishes of Mrs Thatcher
herself. His role was variously seen as that of the loyal
servant, the family solicitor, the barrister with his brief, or,
more crudely, the man who always does, or tries to do, what
the boss wants. He was also subjected to a number of
humiliating rebuffs by the Prime Minister at private meetings
of ministers and officials.

Howe had become disillusioned with incomes policy
through his practical experience under Heath. The monetarists, too, were against incomes policies on pragmatic
grounds; but they were also against them on principle (cf.
'Memorial to the Prime Minister'). Their objection to incomes
policies on principle had two roots. First, their economic
theory told them that incomes policies were either irrelevant
or damaging (they would control inflation by controlling the
money supply); second, they saw incomes policies as yet
another extension of the intervention they so abhorred on
ideological grounds. For Conservatives who felt that under
Heath the legal route (the Industrial Relations Act and the
statutory incomes policy) to tame the unions and end
inflation had failed lamentably, monetarism was the panacea
offered when orthodox medicine has no cure. First, it said
(all monetarists said) that inflation was caused by excessive
monetary growth and could be cured by not having excessive
monetary growth. Secondly, it said (most monetarists said)
that incomes policies were irrelevant to the inflationary
process: either they didn't work, or, if they did work, what
they achieved was alleviation of unemployment – stopping
so many people from pricing themselves out of work through
excessive wage claims. Thirdly, it said (some monetarists
said) – following on from the second part – that unions did
not cause inflation at all (that was done by governments);
they merely caused unemployment through those excessive

wage claims. Fourthly, in addition to being ineffectual, incomes policies were positively harmful, because they distorted differentials between wage rates, and hence the working of the market place (it was difficult to reconcile the objection that incomes policies distorted differentials with the objection that they did not work).

In monetarism and its attitudes towards incomes policy we see the several strands of the new economic evangelicalism: there is monetarism itself; there is distaste for incomes policies for allegedly impeding the harmonious workings of unfettered market forces – the right-wing, or economic liberal, or market economist approach; and there is the powerful repugnance towards everything, such as incomes policy, which enhances the role of the state, thereby, it was asserted, posing threats to liberty and freedom.

Eulogies about the golden age of the market place, and warnings about the threat to freedom and liberty from the ever-encroaching state, were to play a recurrent role in the thinking and speeches of Margaret Thatcher and Keith Joseph during the years 1975–79. These economic evangelicals did not accept that the dreaded Keynesians, so far from impeding market forces, might actually have helped them to function better; the market system, by being fettered, to last longer; and real threats to freedom, in the shape of the totalitarian enemy, to be warded off. Nor, in the reflex condemnation of incomes policies per se (as opposed to suggestions that government should learn from their mistakes and try harder to make union policies work better), did they give any weight to the view that incomes policies, if they could assist in the battle against inflation, might actually strengthen the bastions of a 'free' society. It was, after all, the unemployment problem in pre-war Germany, which followed the hyperinflation in Weimar, that provided Adolf Hitler with his stamping ground.

Whereas monetarism tempted its converts with a seductively false precision, the revival of 'liberal' obsessions with the threat to freedom and liberty were characterized by a no less seductive vagueness and ambiguity. After the great historic strides taken in the previous three hundred years in political, religious, economic and social freedom, the pictures conjured up in 1975–79 by the economic liberals about the so-called threat to this freedom showed a certain lack of perspective.

Such noises had been made for some years by the Institute of Economic Affairs. What then was the sudden threat to liberty in the 1970s? For the answer one can reasonably begin with the revival of interest in the writings of Friedrich von Hayek, the Austrian philosopher and economist. In 1945 Hayek, heavily influenced by East European experience, had published a famous apocalyptic warning entitled *The Road to Serfdom* – a work which preceded Orwell's *1984* by four years. No doubt because of the poor political and philosophical productivity of the British workforce, the road to serfdom remained unconstructed in Britain after the war; but this did not mitigate Hayek's worries, which resurrected themselves in less palpable form in *Constitution of Liberty* in 1962.

Hayek's works were much cited by the economic evangelicals during the period 1974–79. What events were they reacting to, as tangible signs that liberty in Britain was being threatened? One was the growing power, as they perceived it, of organized labour. Another was the reaction of government to this: Heath had invited the unions in to share the reins of economic policy-making; and even while Sir Keith and his colleagues were formulating their alternatives to Heath-style policies in 1974–75, the Labour government seemed to be leaning over backwards to please the trade unions, and accede to their demands.

During this same 1974–75 period, the chickens of the previous two years were coming home to roost. Inflation rose to a post-war peak of 26 per cent per annum, prompting considerable, and entirely understandable, alarm. In addition to the reasons adduced in the last chapter for this inflationary surge, the pressures had continued under Labour: after the breakdown of Heath's incomes policy, Labour promised, and introduced, a period of 'free collective bargaining', with the result that wage settlements escalated dramatically. The new administration also allowed the 'threshold' wage indexation system to continue for a time. Before very long, therefore, in the summer of 1975, the country found itself back with an incomes policy as the major part of a serious attempt to get inflation under control once more.

These were the years of the so-called 'social contract', under which the Labour government did its best to placate the TUC in return for cooperation and restraint on wage demands. Both the cooperation and the restraint were figments of politicians' and trade unionists' imaginations until the summer of 1975 (Harold Wilson, the Labour Prime Minister, was determined to allow no unpopular measure through until the referendum on whether Britain should stay in the EEC was safely out of the way in June 1975).

The early period of the social contract was therefore perfect fodder for those who were worried about the alleged tendency towards a corporate state. After that, although the unions began to cooperate with the government in trying to control wage increases and in bringing the inflation rate down, they continued to be offered a share — or at least a semblance of a share — in economic policy-making. In the early period the right wing and the economic liberals in the Tory Party were worried about the continuation of accelerating inflation and the trend, as they saw it, towards a corporate state. In the latter period (1976 onwards) inflation may have been coming down, but the price of cooperation with organized labour was considered too heavy and dangerous a cost to bear in terms of 'freedom'.

The glib use of the term 'corporate state' was a conscious evocation of Mussolini's Italy and even Hitler's Germany. It was designed to draw attention to the threat to parliamentary democracy if Parliament was by-passed and 'deals' struck between the new 'robber barons' of the trade unions, and ministers.

There were strong grounds for believing that Labour ministers overreached themselves in their enthusiasm to offer concessions to the unions during this period — union leaders have been heard to say since that they were offered far more than they were asking for. But the parallels intended to be evoked by the phrase 'corporate state' were always far-fetched.

One of the oddities of these objections to governmental attempts to make organized labour behave more responsibly is conjured up by the memory of pre-war Austria. One of the elements in the rise of Nazism there had been the attempt to crush the unions. After the war, Austria pursued a largely successful policy of giving organized labour a share in the reins of control, especially of economic management.

Again, there were two ways of looking at the governmental attempts to work with the unions during this 'social contract' phase. One was the economic liberals' spectre of robber barons threatening to crush the democratic process. Another view, well argued by Robert Taylor in *The Fifth Estate* (1978), is that the robber barons were actually rather weak. One of the problems with the way organized labour has evolved in Britain is that it is scattered and fragmented, competing with itself and not sufficiently controlled from the centre. In a sense, trade union behaviour in Britain in the 1970s had been a model of unfettered, competitive nine-teenth-century economic liberalism; government and central trade union leaders, for a time, joined forces to try to bring some order into the system. The economic liberals so concerned about 'cooperation' wanted to eschew such attempts, advocating instead a strong, centrally directed effort to control the money supply, come what may. Faced with the objection that the Bank of England did not think it an easy job to control the money supply in such a complex economy and society as modern Britain, Peter Jay in *The Times* resorted to crying that the Bank of England should be directed to do so through the medium of a new institution, a Currency Commission.

If the 'corporatist' fear was vague and intangible as proof of encroachment of the public sector and threats to liberty, another great fear of the economic liberals was considered much less imprecise at the time. This was the size of the public sector: right-wing concern about public spending was always with us, even during the heyday of Macmillan and Butskellism. But when the Treasury announced that public expenditure was approaching 60 per cent of the gross domestic product early in 1976, the fears spread far beyond the right wing. Such respected middle-of-the-road figures as

Roy Jenkins were to be heard saying that the trend of spending posed a threat to democracy.

Yet those figures turned out to be a hoax, albeit an unwitting one. The Treasury and the Government Statistical Service, which pride themselves – for all the jokes at their expense – on their statistical purity, had to admit that they had got the figure wrong, double-counted certain items, and grossly overstated the proportion. (A full explanation is contained in Sir Leo Pliatzky's book *Getting and Spending*, which put the revised proportion at 47 per cent in 1976, not 60 per cent.) Nevertheless, public spending was a good Aunt Sally. It was always easy to find specific examples of profligacy; it was seldom difficult to generalize on the subject.

Worries and fears about the high level of public spending and the threat to freedom from state encroachment were to become predominant themes of speeches by Margaret Thatcher and Sir Keith Joseph during the 1975–79 period. And within the Tory party the debate, and preparation for the election, were to proceed at two levels. One level was the formal machinery of the Tory Party research and committee network, where policy, although heavily influenced by the thinking and demands of the economic evangelicals, still had to compromise at certain points with the views of the non-evangelicals – the men whom Mrs Thatcher was later to christen the 'wets'. The second level – one might fairly say the more strident level – was that of the economic evangelicals on their own account: speeches, perhaps under the auspices of the Centre for Policy Studies, and meetings of the faithful alone. This second level was important for keeping the pure spirit of the counter-revolution undiluted and fresh.

The continued existence of the formal structure served the purpose, conscious or unconscious, of diverting the more middle-of-the-road Tories from what was really going on. Equally important, perhaps, they simply did not want to know or believe the strength of the burgeoning faith. Yet it was all there in the speeches of Margaret Thatcher and Sir Keith Joseph – particularly of the latter. What was being advocated was nothing less than the abandonment of the post-war consensus between Conservative and Labour over the centre ground and common aspirations of politics.

The Preston speech had concentrated on monetarism and employment policies. That in Hull had eminently confirmed Sir Keith's fears that it might prove a political boomerang. But that was only the beginning of Sir Keith's campaign. And the mistake of his opponents was to infer that because he had lost the leadership election, his views could accordingly be dismissed: for Sir Keith's views were also Margaret Thatcher's views. The difference between them was that Mrs Thatcher did not need to undergo an intellectual's 'agonizing reappraisal'. It was not for nothing that the two were respectively christened 'the Mad Monk' and 'the Blessed One' by their colleagues in the Shadow Cabinet. Whereas Sir Keith gave the impression that he had suddenly seen the light, Mrs Thatcher behaved for all the world as if she had been basking in it all along. There was no mystery about Mrs Thatcher's relationship with economic evangelicalism, as she made clear whenever she gave unscripted answers in television and radio interviews. She as good as boasted to the world that she was born into a family of economic evangelicals and was proud of it. It so happened that the goals and values being discovered by Sir Keith were strongly reminiscent of Mrs Thatcher's girlhood memories: 'Victorian virtues' of industry and thrift; a commonsense and unsophisticated belief that the nation should balance its books like the household (or like some platonic 'ideal' type of the Victorian household) – these were the kinds of attributes which were common to the growing circle around Mrs Thatcher from 1975 onwards, for whose members her simple question was: 'Is he one of us?'

Thus Mrs Thatcher had no need of a sudden conversion. She had demonstrated great intelligence and dedication in her career as a research chemist and tax barrister; but suggestions by her biographers that she had been wrestling with the ideas of Hayek since 1945 seem rather far-fetched. 'She was much more at home with the simple homespun philosophy of William Simon,' said one of her close colleagues at the time. (William Simon, US Treasury Secretary during the time of the Labour government's negotiations with the International Monetary Fund in 1976, subsequently wrote a characteristically evangelical book about his economic philosophy.)

Mrs Thatcher in the mid 1970s can be seen as a simple provincial girl looking for an uncomplicated philosophy. Sir Keith Joseph gave it to her; and after that she broadened her circle of faithful advisers. She had regular meetings with like-minded businessmen such as John Hoskyns, who had built up a successful computer business, Norman Strauss of Unilever, and others. Her rediscovery of her basic values made Mrs Thatcher a poacher-turned-gamekeeper when it came to the general subject of public spending, as opposed to specific spending on education when she was a departmental minister. She was never a monetarist as such; nor, for that matter, was she particularly versed in economics. But an economic philosophy which put 'sound money' above all else was an obvious attraction to her; while other sections of the Shadow Cabinet and the research department were attempting to keep the monetarist faction in the party under some sort of control in 1975–79, Mrs Thatcher made a point of trying to immerse herself in the subject, having private sessions with a number of the newly fashionable economists.

Meanwhile what Sir Keith Joseph did in his series of speeches at that time was not only to spell out his own thinking on the state of the economy and the nation: it was also to rationalize the deepest instincts and prejudices of Mrs Thatcher herself. His opponents were inclined to dismiss Sir Keith too glibly as 'the Mad Monk'. But these supposedly cloistered thoughts had an influence on the attitudes of the inner circle of the Tory Party which does much to explain the way they handled – or mishandled – the problems in office.

The 1975–79 period of Tory opposition can be seen as being as significant, in its own way, as the 1945–51 period. The difference was that the weight of intellectual and political ethos was pulling in the opposite direction to what was experienced in 1945–51. Whereas R. A. Butler and his colleagues had done their best, with considerable success, to swing the party towards the centre, Sir Keith Joseph and Margaret Thatcher were equally determinedly swinging it back towards the right.

This very process begged the predominant question of post-war Conservative politics: could a party so dependent on working-class support – a party which had probably lost the 1945 election because of the workers' distrust of its intentions and memories of the 1930s – *afford* to be seen to be moving to the right? Would such a step – or series of steps – not be taken as indicating a desire for political suicide?

One answer to this was that the 1970s were a long way from the 1930s; many of the electorate with first-hand memories of those years had died; a new generation was writing about the period from written sources only, and with suitable blinkers could argue that the unhappiness of the depression years was largely a myth (a good example of the need for the oral tradition, because there were still enough people alive in the 1970s whose families had suffered from the unemployment and heartless application of the means test during that period).

Another answer was that if sufficient emphasis was put on the attractive aspects of a move to the right, the electorate might be wooed, and diverted from the less pleasing implications of the policy shift. In this regard, there was ample ground on which to build up a consensus between the various wings of the Tory Party, which would also have electoral appeal. This was in a re-emphasis of that basic theme of post-war Conservative policies which even – perhaps especially – under Macmillan and Butler had met with considerable electoral success.

At any one time, faced with any particular set of economic constraints, the 'wetter' members of the Tory Party will always tend to favour lower taxation and lower public expenditure than the Labour Party. And given a choice between more direct taxation and more indirect taxation, the Tories will incline towards raising the latter. Even those members of the electorate whose attitudes towards the Tories are most scarred by memories of the 1920s and 1930s are likely to favour lower taxes for themselves – especially if these can be found from the elimination of those universal scourges, waste and bureaucracy in the public sector.

These themes were to be developed with considerable harmony in front of a willingly rapt audience as the election approached. Much of the emphasis in economic policy was going to be placed on lower taxation and on savings in public expenditure; and in electoral speeches the targets for savings – other than the bogy of 'waste and inefficiency' – were to be left suitably vague. Indeed, certain important pledges were to be given on the protection of some of the welfare sacred cows, such as pensions.

But the tenor of Sir Keith Joseph's speeches was very different. There were no concessions to the virtue of retaining a foothold on the middle ground. On the contrary; it was the Tory attempt to compete for the middle ground which was responsible for many of the economic problems now facing the country. That middle ground was a veritable bed of nettles which an incoming Tory administration would have to bend down and grasp.

Sir Keith's central point was that the Tories, the economy, and the country were suffering from a 'ratchet effect'. Instead of fighting for what they knew to be right – or ought to have known: Sir Keith freely beat his breast in an effort to expiate his sins for having belonged to earlier administrations which contributed to the ratchet effect – previous Tory governments had made too many concessions to the left.

Sir Keith's analysis led him to argue that the central preoccupation of the Tory Party of Butler and Macmillan was misconceived: by searching always for the middle ground, the Tories were allowing the rules to be dictated by their opponents. It was as if – this is my analogy for Sir Keith's argument, not his – the centre spot in a football match had been progressively moved by your opponents into your own half, and was now somewhere around the penalty area. As each goal was scored, each point lost, the match continued with the kick-off point placed very much to your opponents' advantage. The distilled views of Hayek could be discerned, as it were, on the touchline of this analysis. So could the prophecies of the economic historian Joseph Schumpeter, who had warned that his beloved capitalism contained the seeds of its own evolution into socialism.

Sir Keith took various common sources of complaint at the time – the size of the public sector, the potential enervation of entrepreneurial initiative, the endless subsidies for the nationalized industries and failing private industries – and attributed them to the ratchet effect. The implication of his analysis was that the preoccupation with the middle ground had to be abandoned, in the national interest. Given that this revolutionary teaching had devastating implications for the old post-war assumptions about Tory electoral strategy, both the national and the Tory interest dictated the need for a new approach. So the Tories needed to change their clothes if they were to regain the position of power from which to change the country's direction.

Sir Keith's analysis raised fundamental questions about the concept of Conservatism. And if there is one thing certain about the concept of Conservatism, it is that it means different things to different people – even, at different times, to the same people.

We referred earlier (Chapter One) to the Disraeli tradition, and the distinction between the reactionary, who opposes all change, and the Disraeliite, who wants to preserve what is best of the British tradition and constitution, but to make necessary reforms and even to anticipate the trend or pace of reform. In this sense, Macmillan, author of The Middle Way in the 1930s, was in the Disraeli tradition; so were R. A. Butler and the late Iain Macleod. It is the opinion of many Disraeliites that the party's move to the right would never have occurred if Macleod had not died so tragically young.

One way of examining Sir Keith's position is to bear in mind that it is an analysis which could have been made – indeed was made, in different words – on many occasions during the previous hundred years. Thus the ratchet effect was certainly operating at the turn of the century when the new Liberals began to oppose the nineteenth-century economic liberals so beloved of Sir Keith and his followers. What could be more of a ratchet, a departure from the centre, than (in Leonard Hobhouse's words in 1904) the suggestion that

It is for the State to take care that the economic conditions are such that the normal man who is not defective in mind or body or will can by useful labour, feed, house and clothe himself and his family. The 'right to work' and the right to a 'living wage' are just as valid as the right of person or property.

In that battle during the first decade of the century, the Liberal Party – threatened by the approach to the centre ground of both the Tories and the new Labour Party – had allowed the new Liberals to triumph over the older Liberals in crying that the respect for the freedom of the individual must be tempered by some collective effort to help those who could not help themselves. Such 'collective' efforts were to lead to a greater degree of 'freedom' for many more individuals, so that the concern with the freedom of the individual may not, in the event, have been required at all. But many old Liberals thought at the time that this was a dangerous move into the middle ground.

What Sir Keith advocated, and what was to have some impact in the propaganda war, was a search for common ground: the Tories, he argued, should decide firmly what they stood for. Clearly, one thing he wanted them to stand for was the abandonment of the middle ground; and they should get people to agree on what were common objectives and what policies were acceptable by all sides.

There was no getting away from it, though, however skilfully Sir Keith presented his analysis: abandoning the middle ground of the post-war consensus on economic policy, and attacking the size of the public sector and the welfare state, meant that the search for common ground was running into trouble before, as it were, it could get off the ground. Much of the common ground was inevitably being abandoned with the middle ground.

This created tension in the Tory research department, the source of much of the material for speeches and talks which a Shadow Cabinet draws on. Despite the new broom which had swept through Central Office after Mrs Thatcher assumed

the leadership, the intellectual furniture was much the same:
a handful of hard-worked researchers and advisers such as
Chris Patten (later to become Tory MP for Bath in the 1979
general election) and Adam Ridley (later to be the Chancellor's political adviser) provided much of the material
required by the Shadow Cabinet. Although Ridley was in the
process of becoming a disillusioned Keynesian, he had
certainly not undergone the kind of 'road to Damascus'
conversion experienced by Sir Keith. Nor, a fortiori, had
Chris Patten, who remained both a Keynesian and a stout
believer in the social, economic and political advantages of
being positioned in the middle ground. Both Ridley and
Patten saw an important part of their role as being that of
'damage limitation'. They were servicing people who knew
– or thought they knew – about the economy, such as Sir
Keith Joseph and Margaret Thatcher; people who were
learning about the economy, such as Sir Geoffrey Howe; and
Shadow ministers who were not necessarily knowledgeable
or trying very hard to learn, but who had to go through the
motions of referring to the economy in their speeches.

Since there was not much sympathy for the
Joseph/Thatcher view of the world among the majority of the
Shadow Cabinet, the material they received was uncontrov-
ersial. But a lot of the time and energy in the research
department in those years was devoted to shooting down
what were regarded as the wilder ideas floated by Sir Keith
and Mrs Thatcher – ideas which, to paraphrase one of the
Cambridge philosopher Dr Kasimir Lewy's favourite remarks,
'might seem far-fetched, but had been fetched from no farther
than the new Centre for Policy Studies round the corner'.

But this is not to suggest that it was a straight fight between
the research department and the monetarists. People like
Ridley were typical of a number of economists who were
undergoing the agonies of having been educated in the
Keynesian tradition, but worrying about the appropriateness
of the Keynesian prescription, particularly to an economy
with the severe problem that many people thought con-
fronted the British economy at the time. For an important
influence on the views of the Tories at this time was the

traumatic experience the Labour government was having in 1976 at the hands of the International Monetary Fund and foreign creditor governments, notably the US. The Labour Cabinet had started to try to put its house in order with the incomes policy introduced in the summer of 1975, but the fall in the pound after 4 March 1976 represented an old-style collapse of confidence, which the Cabinet spent the best part of the year trying to redress. This involved difficult cuts in public expenditure to appease both the financial markets and the US Treasury – particularly the US Treasury Secretary, William Simon, who was an economic evangelical if ever there was one.

It was during 1976, under the Labour administration, that monetarism was able to establish a bridgehead in Britain. What the Tories did in 1979 was to continue a campaign, with much greater vigour, using weapons with which the Treasury and Bank of England provided them in 1976. The essential difference was that before 1979 few knowledgeable observers believed there was much more than a monetarist tinge to the economic policies of the British government. After May 1979 monetarism was to move to the centre of the stage, and other important levers of policy to be abandoned. But the path towards monetarism had certainly been laid.

An overridingly difficult question for the Labour administration under Prime Minister James Callaghan and Chancellor Denis Healey was what importance to attach to the new-found interest in monetarism. The City and the financial markets were obsessed by it; the press, in the shape of many of the leading commentators, was also obsessed by it. And a number of influential officials in the Treasury and Bank of England – including the Governor, Gordon Richardson, himself – were also paying much more sympathetic attention to the monetarists than they had in the early 1970s. The big policy question was: just how much importance should be attached to monetarism both as an indication of what was going wrong with the British economy and as a solution?

An important factor in this painful struggle was the debilitated state of morale among the Keynesian economic establishment who still held the dominant positions in

Whitehall and the Bank. The circumstances of their resort to the IMF and the conditions demanded by the US Treasury were humiliating. The establishment was not in prime fighting condition to take on the monetarists, who rightly sensed that they were in the ascendancy. The Bank of England, for instance, was sufficiently desperate at this time to suggest publicly that there should be a fixed target for the growth of national income (in money terms) each year, and that it should be left to society – in effect the unions – to decide, through their behaviour over wage demands, how much should be absorbed by wages, and how much by output. This implied that no attempt should be made to contain the rise in unemployment if the money supply expanded at above a certain rate. It was a more explicit threat of unemployment than had hitherto been used by British governments.

Perhaps the nadir of the fortunes of the Keynesian economic establishment was signified by the widespread attention devoted in the monetarist literature, at the time and for some years after, to a speech by James Callaghan at the Labour Party conference of September 1976. In this speech Callaghan appeared to disavow any lingering belief in the efficiency of traditional demand management. 'You cannot spend your way out of recession,' he averred in a notorious passage. The speech attracted much attention at the time among the active Tory monetarists such as Sir Keith Joseph, John Biffen, Nigel Lawson and Jock Bruce-Gardyne. It has not only been quoted many times since by the economic evangelicals; it has been skilfully built on, as a foundation for some of the very clever arguments the Thatcher government was going to employ in justification of its policies. We shall see this in more detail later: for the moment it will suffice to remind the reader of the oft-repeated assertion in 1979/82 that 'there is no alternative' – summarized by the letters 'Tina', an acronym often used in Westminster to refer to Mrs Thatcher, who was one of the most frequent users of the argument.

Given the importance which has been attached to that speech, it is worth reflecting on the circumstances in which it was made. For one thing, the Labour government was in the midst of another crisis of confidence in the pound – a crisis which caused Denis Healey, the Chancellor, to 'turn back at the airport' (instead of flying to Manila for the IMF annual conference, Healey was persuaded that he had better stay in London and put the British economic house in order). Callaghan's speech was made at a time when the financial markets – the holders of sterling – were panicking, and in an atmosphere where monetarism had taken a strong hold.

Callaghan was therefore trying to appease the markets by telling them what they wanted to hear. He was also trying to frighten the Labour Party – in this instance, both the annual conference, then in progress, and his fellow Cabinet ministers. And in doing both these things he was hoping to make an impression on the Secretary to the US Treasury, William Simon, that he was serious about offering British financial rectitude in return for a US-backed IMF loan to help the UK out of its temporary financial problems. In other words, the speech was more a tactical move than a full and serious reappraisal of policy – although it suited Callaghan and Healey at the time to cultivate the latter view.

But the speech undoubtedly represented a *partial* reappraisal of policy. It was intended to acknowledge that if inflation was accelerating, and /or the financial markets were panicking, a British government would be wise to concentrate on getting the inflation under control, and would in any case not be allowed to attempt otherwise by the financial markets. There is all the difference in the world between advocating expansionary measures when inflation is 25 per cent per annum and accelerating, and when it is 10 per cent and falling, and unemployment is 3 million and rising. Moreover, the tactical situation facing Callaghan was complicated by the feelings of panic and irrationality that tend to permeate the atmosphere during times of sterling crisis. Participants in, and sufferers from, such crises sometimes get the impression that it is not enough to satisfy foreign creditors by putting your house in order: they almost seem to want to knock the house down and rebuild it. Against such a reaction, Callaghan could in turn be forgiven for himself over-reacting.

As a tactical move, the Callaghan speech was successful, although its true significance did not become fully apparent at the time. It was that speech which enabled the pro-British element in the US administration – who were concerned that Callaghan might fall and that there could be a violent lurch to the left in Britain – to persuade Simon of the US Treasury that the British government meant business. But its hyperbolic and misleading element from the point of view of subsequent developments was its logical leap from the suggestion that old-style demand management was inappropriate in certain circumstances to the view first that it was inappropriate in all circumstances, and second that it had never worked anyway. These latter elements were pure assertion. From the tactical point of view, however – vis-à-vis both the Labour Party and opinion abroad – such oratorical flourishes suited Callaghan's short-term political purpose.

The message would also have sat quite happily in Sir Keith Joseph's Preston speech of two years earlier. But as a basis for such major policy prescriptions as it was used – or advanced – for in the early 1980s, Callaghan's speech was somewhat flimsy. Recognition of this flimsiness was implicit in a number of speeches Callaghan was to make for the opposition benches in the early 1980s, when Mrs Thatcher and her colleagues were preaching that there was no alternative to existing policies.

I have left until last the point most often made about this speech: namely that at the time Callaghan was under the monetarist influence of his son-in-law, Peter Jay (this was before Jay's appointment to Washington as British Ambassador, when he was still economics editor of The Times). Indeed, I understand that Jay drafted the passage himself. It is not difficult to assess who was using whom most; the message was certainly immediately useful to Callaghan, but it served the monetarist cause for years to come.

This brings us to the role of the Bank of England in the rise of monetarism. The Bank, like the Conservative Party, had a reputation to live down in the post-war world. Its attitude to unemployment during the 1920s under Montagu Norman was insensitive, reprehensible, and, once Keynes and Ernest Bevin had got to work cross-examining Norman on behalf of the Macmillan Committee, open. Central banks have a natural bias in favour of 'sound money' in any conflict of objectives with unemployment. But, this said, the attitude of the post-war nationalized Bank of England – particularly under the governorship of Leslie O'Brien and Gordon Richardson – has been much more understanding of the wider economic and social issues involved. Indeed, it was for a long time during the 1970s a common criticism levelled by monetarists that the Bank of England was, if anything, the last bastion of Keynesianism.

During the early seventies the Bank was much criticized in the City and by monetarist commentators for not taking monetarism seriously enough; for not controlling the money supply; even for being anti-monetarist. However, as worries about inflation grew, the Bank, under the prodding of Gordon Richardson, began to react to these criticisms. One response – the idea floated (and referred to above) of a target for 'money national income' – did not really get off the ground. Bank thinking then began to favour the adoption of a target rate of growth for the money supply itself: even if the Bank did not fully accept the monetarist case, a number of officials of both Bank and Treasury argued that the publication of a target for monetary growth might at least concentrate people's minds, and force greater attention on the counter-inflation battle. Denis Healey, as Chancellor, became very enthusiastic about the idea, and the Labour government – trying everything to appease the financial markets and restore confidence – began to publish targets for the money supply after the 1976 financial crisis.

As it turned out, the Callaghan/Healey administration was too successful by half in reassuring the financial markets. British and international investors began to switch investments back into pounds, and by the autumn of 1977 the upward pressure on the pound became very strong.

One of the subjects of particular interest to the IMF in the

1976 loan negotiations had been the value of the pound and the competitiveness of British exports. Overvaluation of the pound in 1974–75 was deemed both by the IMF and by the British Keynesian economic establishment to have been the principal cause of the balance of payments problems of those years. The IMF thought a sterling /dollar rate of about $1.70 was appropriate. But in the autumn of 1977 the pound was tending to shoot up strongly, and was only being held back by massive Bank of England intervention in the exchange market. In such circumstances the Central Bank can supply its own currency, in this case pounds, for foreign exchange, thereby limiting the degree to which the strong demand for pounds is driving up the exchange rate.

Now monetarists tend not to like such intervention. Apart from anything else, it clashes with their belief in the wisdom of market forces, and their disinclination to 'second guess' those market forces. The Bank of England has traditionally been more inclined to intervene in the exchange market – critics would even argue that it was trigger-happy. 'Market forces may work in the long run, but the markets tend to over-react in the short run, and we have access to more information than they do' was the way one veteran Bank man put it to me.

Moreover, in this case the Bank was in a dilemma. The extra influx of funds into the country was swelling the monetary figures and making it virtually certain that the official target would be exceeded by a wide margin. For those who believed the monetarist thesis that there was a direct causal relationship between increases in the money supply and subsequent inflation, the inference was obvious. Others were tempted by the argument that a higher exchange rate would bring direct relief on prices, and hence help the general battle against inflation.

As so often happens with economic policy when market pressures are involved, the decision was taken in haste at a meeting of ministers and Treasury and Bank officials at No. 10 Downing Street. One background factor in the air was a theory advocated by (among others) some economists at the London Business School that the Keynesian orthodoxy about exchange rates was ill founded, and that a strong exchange rate policy was preferable to what was regarded as the treadmill of devaluation, followed by wage explosion.

Whether or not the Bank of England had fully accepted monetarist doctrine – which is very doubtful – it had certainly campaigned for monetary targets and put its prestige behind them. Its advice was that, since it had come to a choice between the money supply targets and the exchange rate, the latter would have to give. This advice was accepted by the government.

Both incidents – the adoption of published monetary targets and the decision to allow the pound to float up to protect those monetary targets – were milestones on the road towards the Thatcher administration's monetarism. Whether they were 'monetarist' decisions is another question. There was an inclination when the morale of the Keynesian establishment became low to try almost anything. 'Monetarism' is a commitment to a particular brand of monetary policy above all else. In the winter of 1978–79 the Labour government, if it ever had such a commitment, was to throw it to the winds in a vain electioneering attempt; so any commitment was not to last very long, and to prove skin-deep. The 'true' monetarists were always suspicious of the semblance of monetarism under Labour, and frequently used the term 'unbelieving monetarism'. But 1977 was certainly the year when the rot set in. The Healey period at the very least saw a flirtation with monetarism, and that flirtation made an important contribution to the change in policy towards the exchange rate. For, as we shall see later, it was via the exchange rate that monetarism was to wreak its real damage in the Thatcher years.

The change in attitude towards the exchange rate was a reaction of some of the disillusioned Keynesians. It was at a time when some economists started to argue: 'These policies never got us anywhere; let us try those policies.' In the case of the exchange rate, the prescriptions of the London Business School registered a remarkable about-turn.

For many years it had been an accepted tenet of economic policy that exchange rates have to be adjusted from time to time to reflect differing inflation rates. I have already referred to the crisis created in the 1920s by the return to the Gold Standard at too high an exchange rate: Britain suffered a deeper depression than that experienced in the rest of the world. During the mid sixties, although the Wilson administration staved off devaluation for a time, economists within Whitehall were almost unanimous in crying that this was a mistake. But in the 1970s a reaction set in. Some economists argued that depreciation of the currency got the country nowhere, because wage-earners soon cottoned on to the fact that their 'real' wages – that is, after allowing for higher prices – were being eroded by the higher import prices that inevitably followed a devaluation. Some studies suggested that, after a period of years, the putative 'advantage' of the devaluation for industry's competitiveness was whittled away.

It is important to stress here that the full effect of the 'catching-up' process did take a number of years. But this did not stop some monetarists and disillusioned Keynesians from seizing on the research and either distorting it or misunderstanding it. It was an easy leap to conclude that devaluation did no good at all; and it was but a short further leap to argue that it was positively harmful, because it caused prices to rise, and that was bad, was it not? And so it came about that depreciation of the currency's external value was branded 'inflationary'.

It was, of course; but to react against all depreciations was to misunderstand the mechanism. There is a difference between depreciation when other things are equal, and depreciation when they are not. If a country's inflation rate is not out of line with that in other countries, and its exports are reasonably competitive, then a depreciation is unnecessary for trade and employment, and will aggravate the inflation rate. But if a country is suffering rising unemployment because its industries cannot compete on equal terms against other countries – because inflation has driven wage costs too high – then an adjustment has to be made if the relative employment position is not going to remain weak, or even deteriorate further. This is to compensate for *past* inflation, to allow the external value of the currency to come into line with the internal value.

However, the new enthusiasts for a strong exchange rate tried to turn the conventional arguments on their head. They pointed to such strong currency countries as Germany and Japan, noted their good industrial performance, and argued that we in Britain too could improve our economic performance if we escaped from the cycle of depreciation and opted for a strong exchange rate instead.

A more impressive argument from the strong exchange rate school was that it would be much better not to have the kind of inflation Britain tended to suffer, so that there would be no need to undergo the debilitating traumas often associated with periodic devaluations. This was fairly unexceptionable, and in accordance with the goals of most other economists. But the point was that, if competitiveness had already been lost via too large an increase in wage costs, relative to those of other countries, then it made more sense to aim to restore that competitiveness via an exchange rate depreciation, than to make the situation worse via a higher exchange rate.

There can be little doubt that, in the past, Keynesians and others had been too cavalier about the exchange rate. This was especially true, as we have seen, in 1972 when the pound was allowed to float down. British policy went from one extreme – a tendency towards holding the exchange rate too high – to another – an excessively relaxed attitude towards how far it should fall. But although both of these were extreme positions, the way the exchange rate was to be allowed to rise at the end of the decade was to put earlier displays of extremism into perspective.

What became clear from the experiences of the early 1970s was that some economists had become too enthusiastic about the possibilities attendant on an escape from the straitjacket of a fixed exchange rate. The effect of a falling exchange rate on import prices – and later on wage claims – served to remind people that the fundamental problem was domestic inflationary forces. Under a fixed exchange rate system these showed up in a balance of payments crisis, as British producers became less competitive, and the economy sucked in too many imports. Flexible exchange rates proved to be no substitute for tackling domestic inflationary pressures at source: but a falling exchange rate could alleviate, and ultimately redress, the unemployment effects of lost competitiveness. One further important point: to the layman it seems curious that anyone should advocate a lower exchange rate. This is understandable. There is an association in people's minds between weakness of currency and weakness of country or political system. Currencies can easily be seen as a natural national virility symbol. But, as with other virility symbols, they can be misinterpreted. The non-swimmer's venture into deep water before an admiring crowd can be a short-lived demonstration of virility. Many a government has, out of a mistaken sense of national pride, made the mistake of hoisting its colours to an unjustifiably high exchange rate, only to have to haul them down in humiliating fashion later.

Again, the layman naturally thinks that a strong pound means he can buy French wine, or Spanish holidays, or Japanese cassette recorders cheaper than before: what is so wrong about that? The answer is: 'Not much up to a point; but things can easily get out of hand.' It sounds fair to increase your spending power in this way. But, to take the argument to its extreme: what happens to a country's spending power in the long run if its industries, the seedcorn of the employment and spending power of a large proportion of the population, collapse because they cannot compete with industries abroad? Clearly, there has to be a happy medium. Certain countries are particularly good at manufacturing certain products, so that there are mutual benefits from an economic system in which countries specialize in those products they are good at, and trade some of them for others in which they do not have such a natural advantage. But if this process gets too distorted, the employment consequences in some countries become intolerable.

Another point which needs emphasizing is that an appropriate exchange rate is only one of a number of necessary conditions for reasonable economic performance. Competitiveness depends on a host of factors, such as the quality and quantity of the stock of capital (factories, machines, and so on); the pace and quality of technological innovation; the ability (in aptitudes and basic skills) to adapt, so that these technological innovations can be exploited; the willingness to respond to changing patterns of demand in the world; and so on. The point about the exchange rate is that all these fundamental conditions will be made that much more difficult to achieve if the country's industries cannot compete on costs.

A final point that is often overlooked: although 'cheaper imports' sounds a good slogan, imports account, on average, for only about a fifth of the total cost of manufacturing in Britain. Wage costs are far and away the most important item. It is possible to envisage assistance in the battle against inflation from a higher exchange rate and cheaper imports. But what is happening on the wages side is more important for manufacturers; and a rise in the exchange rate makes it more difficult – quite apart from all their fundamental competitiveness problems – for them to compete both in export markets and against foreign suppliers in the British market. It is the equivalent of an increase in industrial wage costs, over and above what is negotiated by the unions. It is easy to see that in the struggle to compete, a British manu-facturer suffering from too high labour costs or too high an exchange rate, or both, might be forced to cut his prices – or not to raise them – in order to stay in business. This might ease inflationary pressures in Britain for a while. But in the longer run he needs to restore his profit margins, or he will have to close down some of his factories, or even go out of business.

I have tried to explain these points about the exchange rate at some length, because they were to assume great, if not overriding, importance during the Thatcher experiment.

We have now seen how the economic debate raged while the Tories were in their early years of opposition, and the influences on them. To a certain degree, Labour too was flirting with the new economic ideology, although there are good reasons for thinking that the Labour moves were a tactical diversion. The tensions between the more traditional Tories and the new ideologues had been apparent during what one might call the 'hung opposition' of 1974. Then, with the demise of Heath, Sir Keith Joseph and others had come to the fore: and although the Shadow Cabinet economic policy committee was chaired by somebody who had previously been thought a moderate Tory, namely Sir Geoffrey Howe, Sir Geoffrey himself was gradually being converted to the new religion.

The general tone of Conservative policy for the election was set by *The Right Approach*, published in 1976. But for the economics group the highspot was *The Right Approach to the Economy*, published in October 1977 – just over eighteen months before the 1979 general election.

The significance of 'highspots' depends on one's vantage point. Committees can labour for weeks and months over the wording of a document only to find that most people never get beyond the headlines. The importance of *The Right Approach to the Economy* was that, although there were clearly at least two economic camps in the party, it could be presented as an agreed document – and cited many years afterwards as such. The names on the cover were: Geoffrey Howe, Keith Joseph, David Howell (all, in varying degrees, monetarists) and James Prior. There was also the name of the editor, Angus Maude, who can reasonably be taken as having sympathy with the general approach of the three monetarists.

Many of the fifty-four pages developed familiar themes about the need to 'set the people free' – lower taxation, less government spending and so on – which had been the standard stuff of Tory election manifestos since 1945. Nor can it be argued that monetarism, or high exchange rate policies, actually dominated *The Right Approach to the Economy*. Equally one can sense that the strident and apocalyptic notes in Keith Joseph's speeches were muted in this document signed by others who, in the case of Jim Prior, were very critical of the Joseph approach, and, in the case of Geoffrey Howe, were being advised that there were degrees short of a total break from pre-war policies.

Yet the direction the Thatcher administration was to take

almost immediately it gained office should not necessarily have been a surprise to anyone who had studied *The Right Approach to the Economy.* What would almost certainly have been a surprise was the degree and speed with which they moved. Thus lower government spending to finance direct tax cuts was a firm aim; there was also – given the cost of direct tax cuts – the possibility of higher indirect taxes: 'It may be necessary *in part* to pay for cuts in income tax by higher indirect taxes' (my italics).

There was, for Kremlinologists, a clue to the degree of change in *The Right Approach to the Economy*: 'Our intention is to allow State spending and revenue a *significantly smaller percentage slice* of the nation's annual output and income *each year*' (again, my italics). This was certainly in potential conflict with the gradualism which was meant to characterize the general approach.

The document did not contain the sort of all-out assault on demand management as such that Sir Keith Joseph had made elsewhere. Nor did it say specifically that monetary policy would reign supreme, whatever the consequences for the other economic goals, such as unemployment and the financial health of industry. And it contained fulsome reference to the need for an economic forum at which ministers could discuss the implications of policy – particularly on wages – with both sides of industry.

After proclaiming that 'our prime and overriding objective is to unwind the inflationary coils which have gripped our economy and threaten to throttle the free enterprise system', the document stated: 'We shall aim to continue the gradual reduction in the rate of growth of money supply, in line with firm monetary targets.' And, later, there is a passage taken almost word for word from Sir Keith Joseph's 1974 Preston speech: 'This is not to say that one only has to follow the right money supply path and everything in the economy will become right ... but it is certainly the case that if the management of money is handled wrongly, everything goes wrong.'

Thus the monetarist view of the need for control of the money supply in order to control inflation was imprinted on the document. This primacy was certainly not going to help the subsequent Tory administration in its handling of Britain's intrinsic wage-inflation problem. Indeed, belief, for a time, in the magic mysteries of monetary control was going to turn one of the monetarists' favourite phrases against them and to be an inadequate 'soft option', diverting them from the basic problem.

A number of Tory ministers were going to argue, for some time after the election, that 'Wages do not cause inflation'. One can detect the influence of a steadying hand on the drafters of *The Right Approach to the Economy*, however, because the document did not quite go that far. The repugnance for public sector activity and central government intervention is seen in the passages lambasting incomes policies – although these passages are deftly headed 'a policy for earnings'. Hatred of incomes policy and love of market forces brought the authors to promise a return to 'responsible collective bargaining'. The irresponsibilities of the past were attributed to the inevitable reaction against the distortions caused by earlier incomes policies rather than to what Robert Taylor, in *The Fifth Estate*, has called 'Britain's unique pay bargaining structure'. It was hoped that a policy of strict cash limits for government departments and nationalized industries would keep at bay the irresponsible bargaining tendencies of the past, while in the private sector, strict control of the money supply 'can help to ease the return to realistic collective bargaining'. Also: 'Monetary targets, openly proclaimed and explained, can have a crucial effect in reducing inflationary expectations.'

Before we move on to Part Two, and the policies in practice, it must be emphasized that, if things were to go badly wrong on the inflation front, then a deflationary macroeconomic policy was certainly implied by the public expenditure and monetary policy outlined in *The Right Approach to the Economy*.

And what of that other important strand in this study – the role of the exchange rate? Here too there is a vital clue in *The Right Approach to the Economy*: 'We shall aim . . . to allow our more favourable balance of payments, brought about by the reduced need to import oil, to be reflected in the international value of our currency, initiating a "virtuous circle" of declining inflation.' The justification of this, very much an argument being advanced at the time by two London Business School economists, Alan Budd and Terry Burns, was the bold assertion:

We reject the simplistic argument that a depreciating currency is required to maintain competitiveness. Internal inflation is the real enemy of successful competition. A falling exchange rate makes internal inflation worse. Short-lived gains in price competition are too rapidly eroded for them to bring lasting benefit to the balance of trade.

In common with the emphasis of much of the monetarist academic work of the time, *The Right Approach to the Economy* was relying heavily on the rather nebulous concept of 'expectations' in reducing inflation. We have seen how previous assumptions about the trade-off between inflation and employment went wrong when wage bargainers began trying to compensate for past inflation in their wage demands; in addition, according to the monetarists, they were building in expectations about future inflation. The evidence for this latter assertion, however, is much less well established than what became commonplace in the late 1970s: that wage and salary bargainers at all levels of society felt cheated if their incomes did not at least rise with the recorded inflation rate.

What the Tories were emphasizing in *The Right Approach to the Economy* was first that they wanted to scotch the idea that inflation must continue at prevailing levels; and second that, by progressively reducing monetary growth, they intended to get the inflation rate down: if wage bargainers lowered their sights, inflation *would* come down. And if they did not, then unemployment would result. Much was made in speeches about people 'pricing themselves out of jobs': *The Right Approach to the Economy* merely contained the veiled threat of this, and said:

The monetary authorities will often be subject, directly and indi- rectly, to political and industrial pressures to modify and relax their policies, frequently for reasons of short-term expediency. The dangers of their yielding to such pressure will be reduced if monetary policy is the subject of regular and open public discussion, and if the authorities are expected as a matter of course to give an account of their conduct of policy and of their objectives for the future.

The open discussion was to be at the parliamentary select committee on the Treasury. The document wanted more formal contact between the Bank of England and Parliament; it also said the Tories favoured a more independent role for the Bank, and welcomed 'the trend towards fuller analysis of policy now offered in the Bank's Quarterly Bulletin'. And, for good measure, perhaps the Bank could be represented at the monthly meetings of ministers and both sides of industry in the National Economic Development Council.

With James Prior one of the joint authors, *The Right Approach to the Economy* was muted on the subject of the no man's land of industrial relations. One can divide the worries about the unions into two: behaviour over wage demands, the policy for which we have discussed above; and effects on productivity, via attitudes to change, working practices, and the like.

This subject took up only a page or so of one of the five sections in the fifty-four-page document. Most of this was concerned with the 'closed shop', where the worry expressed was not so much unions as the 'threat to individual freedom'. And even here, all that was being promised was a 'code of conduct':

We recognize that a simple attempt to ban closed shops can be not only ineffective, but sometimes even harmful to some of the individuals concerned. The evidence suggests that informal agreements continue even if formal ones are banned. They may restrict the individual's right to work far more than an open agreement which is regulated and limited.

Truly, then, *The Right Approach to the Economy* suggested that the Tories would tread softly in no man's land. This was clearly under the influence of Prior, and was a major achievement on his part, given the mood of the ascendant

members of the Tory right. Although the document provides
clues to what happened later, it is also true that the concessions to monetarism and economic evangelicalism amounted
to no more than the odd sentence and paragraph. As it turned
out, these were vital parts of the economic evangelicals'
creed; and, like religious doctrinaires, some of the evangelicals were able to quote chapter and verse from *The Right
Approach to the Economy* back at their critics in 1979–83
and declare: 'Well, Jim Prior signed that.' Yet the opponents
of the new religion felt they had done their job by 1979 in
keeping the worst excesses of Sir Keith and Mrs Thatcher at
bay. And, intent on winning the election, the evangelicals
were to make full use of the wets on campaign platforms in
May 1979. The general tone of documents such as *The Right
Approach to the Economy* was much more restrained than
the language of Mrs Thatcher and of her new Employment
Secretary Norman Tebbit was going to prove as time wore on
in 1979–83. The moderate element in the Tory Party in
1978–79 thought they had the evangelicals well under
control. To the extent that the moderates – or 'wets' as Mrs
Thatcher was to christen them – felt that *The Right Approach
to the Economy* contained extreme passages, they felt sure
that experience of government would soon dilute them in
practice. They also thought the theme of 'gradualism' constituted an important victory. In this they did not seem
unjustifiably sanguine at the time. Mrs Thatcher herself
thought the document was 'too wet', and there were no signs
at the time of members of her entourage waving *The Right
Approach to the Economy* in the air and claiming 'We have
outwitted Jim Prior.' The outwitting was to come later.

Part Two

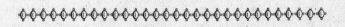

CHAPTER FOUR

ELECTION RUN-UP
AND THE 1979 BUDGET

The publication of *The Right Approach to the Economy* in October 1977 marked the high point of the uneasy consensus between the right wing and the men who came to be known as the 'wets'. It is helpful to remember the obvious point that the wets were and are on the left of the Tory Party, not on the right of the Labour Party. They are by nature more inclined to favour cuts in public expenditure and taxation than, say, the late Anthony Crosland would have done. What was to worry them was the degree to which the economic policies would deviate from the broad Macmillan–Butler tradition of managing demand in order to promote economic growth and employment.

There were important developments between the publication of *The Right Approach to the Economy* and the election which were to change the balance of power in Tory policy even more towards the right. And there was one decision, or non-decision, on the part of Mrs Thatcher which was to contain this move, in practice, despite a much more solid ideological advance.

When Prior was fighting the rearguard action over the attitude towards organized labour in *The Right Approach to the Economy*, the times were partly on his side. The Tories were by now some distance from 1974; and the 1978–79 'winter of discontent' had yet to be experienced. For all the Tory complaints about the distortions and threats to freedom posed by incomes policies, the incomes policies of 1975–76–77 were beginning to produce a better atmosphere in that familiar arena of organized labour. It was in fact the 'free collective bargaining' phase of 1974–75 which produced accelerating inflation and real concern about the irresponsibility of unions. And a theme running through *The Right Approach to the Economy*, oddly enough, is in effect the need to build on certain Labour measures such as the introduction of monetary targets, cash limits for public expenditure, and so on. The summer and autumn of 1977 were the heyday of Denis Healey's Chancellorship, when he was much fêted in Washington at the IMF meeting: Healey was at this time chairman of the IMF's inner policy steering group, the so-called 'Interim Committee'. He was voted one of the top five finance ministers of the year by a New York magazine. And he was even, less than a year after the humiliating events of the autumn of 1976, to be heard preaching to other countries the virtues of putting your financial house in order and going to the IMF for loans and accepting its 'sensible' conditions.

In 1977–78, too, Prime Minister James Callaghan was seeing a lot of the West German Chancellor, Helmut Schmidt, and nurturing aspirations of emulating West Germany's enviable performance in the battle against inflation. Such aspirations were understandable. But West Germany is a society with the advantage of a deep national consensus on the overriding importance of fighting inflation which stems from the reaction to the hyper-inflation of the Weimar Republic; furthermore the West Germans have a much more sensible and less competitive trade union structure than the British – a structure set up after the war, against the background of memories of Weimar, and reflecting the advice of the British TUC on 'how not to do it'.

The state of semi-euphoria in which the Callaghan / Healey economic stewardship found itself was to lure Labour on towards an even more ambitious target for inflation than that implied by *The Right Approach to the Economy*. During the run-up to the 1978–79 wage round, both the arithmetic of the monetary targets and the desire to emulate the German inflation rate led Labour to opt for a wage norm of 5 per cent. This was so far below the 10 per cent which most people regarded as the going rate that it never stood a chance of acceptance by unions or public. Then came the winter of discontent, when the incomes policy was shattered, and there was a series of strikes which damaged both the public image of the unions and Labour's reputation for being able to handle them; this correspondingly hardened public attitudes towards both the unions and the Labour Party. And the failure of an excessively ambitious target for incomes policies led to the discredit of incomes policies as such.

It is a matter for debate whether the British public was voting *for* the Thatcher programme or *against* the tired and somewhat discredited Labour administration. The so-called floating vote is the balance of those voters who change from one party to another, or who come on to the register for the first time (others meanwhile having died), or who vote when they did not vote last time. The size of the floating vote has increased in recent years, and it is a commonplace that the percentage of the total vote going to the winning party has declined over the years.

Certainly, the majority of political commentators seemed to think Labour had made no mean contribution to losing the May 1979 election. But to the extent that the voters were voting *for* the Conservative programme, the question arises: which Conservative programme? The electorate may watch television, read the newspapers, and even glance through the leaflets from their local candidate. It can be stated with confidence that only a minute percentage will have read the manifesto, let alone such fought-over and carefully worded documents as *The Right Approach to the Economy.* If the subtleties of monetarism were to escape many prospective ministers, they were certainly going to be lost on the majority of the electorate.

Election campaigns tend to centre around personalities, the electorate's perception of such personalities (usually gained from television), and fairly simple slogans. More important than the printed manifesto are the impressions people gain of what politicians repeatedly say that they are going to do during the campaign. The spotlight often focuses on a promise or commitment made during the heat of the campaign.

By common consent the Tories did well with their advertising campaign in 1979. The Saatchi and Saatchi slogan 'Labour isn't working', with pictures of 'dole queues' of actors hired to represent some of the 1.3 million unemployed, captured the public imagination. The opposition capitalized with great success on the anti-union feeling of the recent winter. And, during the heat of the campaign, they made what was to prove a rash and expensive promise – to honour the recommendations of the Clegg Commission on public sector pay, which had been set up in an attempt to sort out the chaos created by the breakdown of Labour's 5 per cent pay policy. Nor should we forget the familiar theme of almost all Conservative campaigns since the war: lower taxes and less government expenditure. In the popular mind – and for that matter in the minds of a number of shadow ministers – there was thought to be great scope for lowering public expenditure through the elimination of waste in the public sector, and attacks were made on 'scroungers' who were allegedly drawing unemployment benefit under false pretences. But even at the time it was evident that the campaign commitment on Clegg was in direct contradiction to the Tories' overriding economic promise, in The Right Approach to the Economy and the manifesto, to reduce inflation. The conquest of inflation was the prerequisite of other ambitions to release entrepreneurial initiative and to improve the efficiency of the 'supply side' of the sluggish British economic machine.

Why, then, did Mrs Thatcher make that rash commitment, which virtually guaranteed that the inflation she constantly bemoaned would get much worse before it got better? I asked one of her closest monetarist ministerial colleagues several years later about this: his answer was depressingly simple, but nonetheless interesting, particularly to those students of economic policy who might be confined to ivory towers, or inclined towards an unduly high-minded view of the motivations of our policy-makers: 'Margaret', he said, 'wanted to win that election as if there was no tomorrow.'

There was a tomorrow: the Clegg Commission's findings led to an increase of 25 per cent in the wage bill of the public sector in twelve months. Private sector wage claims shot up in response. And the effect of decisions taken in Sir Geoffrey Howe's first Budget in June 1979 was to combine with the Clegg effect in producing an acceleration in the inflation rate to 21.9 per cent by May 1980, compared with the annual rate of 10.1 per cent inherited by the new government. A Conservative adviser was to comment several years later: 'Although almost every Tory now bewails honouring the Clegg commitment, I have not come across any who dissociated themselves in their election addresses and speeches in May 1979.' What was more, the government ended up honouring not only the handful of public sector claims that had been referred to the Clegg Commission before the election, but many more besides, thereby compounding the problem.

This extraordinarily lax attitude towards the inflationary implications of Clegg may in part be explained by the belief of the evangelicals that in monetarism they had found the Holy Grail. It also owed much to the reaction against incomes policy. Their more conventional economic advisers had argued that, because the government was a large employer in its own right, it required an incomes policy of some sort. But in the run-up to the election and beyond, the evangelicals allowed themselves to believe that, because they were against incomes policy on principle, they would not need one for the public sector – their own employees. If you controlled the money supply you controlled inflation. That was all that mattered.

But we shall examine that first Budget later. The important point to emphasize here is that neither the majority of the electorate nor the majority of the Cabinet quite knew what they were letting themselves in for in May 1979. Nor, for that matter, in a curious way, did anti-union right-wing electors fully appreciate the way the party was going to deal with the unions.

Was unemployment of 3½ million contemplated even in the wildest dreams of the Tories? It is fashionable nowadays to say not. It was certainly neither expected nor advocated by the traditional Tories from whose hands the control of the party's economic policies had been wrested.

What about the monetarists, the economic liberals, the right? The right was certainly hoping for stringent action against the unions. Some of them continued pining for tough anti-union measures, notwithstanding the failure of both the Heath and the Wilson governments to legislate successfully against organized labour in Britain. Some of the monetarists – 'soft' monetarists – had a touching faith in the ability of monetary control to change expectations about inflation quickly and painlessly. Others were less sanguine. My own recollection of talking to the 'hard' monetarists at this time was that, if unemployment had to go on rising until the unions 'saw sense' or were smashed, then their attitude was to shrug their shoulders and say 'That's too bad.' And there was undoubtedly an extreme right-wing element which positively relished the thought of a huge jump in unemployment 'to put the unions in their place'.

But there were, to my knowledge, no predictions of 3 million unemployed being made in the summer of 1979. Statements later, such as that by John Biffen, predicting 'three years of unparalleled austerity', were the closest to capturing the general tenor of what was to come, but such predictions were compatible with a wide range of unemployment figures.

The winter of discontent constituted an important stage between the publication of The Right Approach to the Economy and the application of the new policies. Whether looked at from the viewpoint of Labour losing the election or the Tories winning it, there can be little doubt what impact was made by the events of 1978–79 on the actual election result. But they had another effect too. We have seen that after wresting control of the economic policies of the party, the evangelicals still had to contend with opposition and hard questioning from some of their economic advisers within the official Tory Party organization. We have also seen the role James Prior played in moderating the language about organized labour and the commitment to trade union legislation in *The Right Approach to the Economy*. But the winter of discontent only served to strengthen the hands of the monetarists and the right in the continuing debate within the Tory Party. And it made life even more uncomfortable for disillusioned Keynesians such as Adam Ridley in the research department.

No doubt in reaction to the winter of discontent, the Tory manifesto in 1979 devoted proportionally more space to the unions than had *The Right Approach to the Economy*. But it certainly did not go as far as the evangelicals wanted: they would hardly have volunteered to pen such sentences as 'A strong and responsible trade union movement could play a big part in our economic recovery.'

One of the puzzles for monetarists and the right wing in this context is why, when Mrs Thatcher came into office, she went ahead and made James Prior, who had held the shadow post, Secretary for Employment. A 'tougher' approach to the unions than that likely to come from Prior was surely being called for by the electorate, they argued. But Prior had a strong political base in the party, and for all her apparent radicalism, Mrs Thatcher's closest associates often detected a certain conservatism in her approach to actual decisions. Despite the anti-union atmosphere of the time, the Conservatives went to the polls knowing that over 12 million of the electorate were members of trade unions; although it was clear that many of these wanted modest reforms, the party did not want to frighten these potential voters off with fears that it was about to unleash an unholy war. Despite the fact that the evangelicals were quietly gaining ground, Prior and other moderates were considered vital in the election campaign, to show that the Conservatives were a reasonable, pragmatic, and fairly balanced team. Prior's political weight was acknowledged by the decision to let him assume the Employment portfolio; but the major macro-economic posts were to go, without exception, to the unambiguous believers in the burgeoning economic policy.

Prior was, of course, to prove a considerable irritant to Mrs Thatcher and her believing colleagues. He was exiled to the Northern Ireland Office as soon as the Prime Minister felt sufficiently well established to put Norman Tebbit, one of her devoted acolytes, in the Employment job instead. But in one sense Prior's presence at the Department of Employment did not matter for the monetarists. As it turned out, the element in the party that wanted to best the unions gave them a bigger drubbing through macro-economic policies than they could possibly ever have achieved through specific measures in Parliament. It was assumed that legislation would take many years to have any effect, whereas monetarism managed to cow the unions in a remarkably short time.

But such a policy always looked like a terrible gamble. If one distinguishes between 'behaviour' and 'attitudes', one can see that a return to the atmosphere of the 1920s or 1930s might change the unions' behaviour; but what, in the long run, could it do to their general attitudes? Would it make them more or less cooperative with management and the Tory government that was held responsible for the recession – the rise in unemployment – which had changed their behaviour? There are, for instance, reasonable grounds for believing that part of the explanation for difficult union attitudes in post-war Britain was memories of the slump – just as memories of the way that the means test was actually operated were to hinder political attempts to put the social services on a more economic basis through greater selectivity in the distribution of benefits.

However, before we examine the policy mistakes which were to be made by the Treasury team in the first Budget of June 1979 and subsequently, it is worth regarding the view not only of some adherents of the right, but also of a few disillusioned Keynesians in Whitehall, that the postponement of serious legislation on union questions early in the administration was the most important error of all. After the experience of the previous two administrations in trying to legislate against the unions, this is not a view I would agree with. But I am struck by the forcefulness with which it has been put to me.

One of the men who had held strong views on union problems was John Hoskyns, a man who had achieved the new economic liberal dream of making an enormous financial success of a small company in an expanding area of the market (computer systems). Hoskyns had been struck by the relative dynamism of the US economic system, and felt sufficiently strongly about the British economic problem – which he attributed in no small measure to the unions – to offer his services to the Tories in opposition. Hoskyns got involved in one of the groups of businessmen who attended Tory policy committees in opposition and was invited by Mrs Thatcher to head the policy unit at No. 10 Downing Street when she came into office. We shall take note of some of Hoskyns's influence in due course. In this context, however, it is enough to note that he was one of the most prominent of the minority who felt that a tougher attitude towards the unions should have been maintained right from the beginning, and would happily have fought the entire election on the union issue. (He was not a politician.)

The view put by Hoskyns and a number of monetarist economists was that, as long as the unions possessed monopolistic powers, they would tend to make the employment situation worse for any given level of demand: many of their members would be 'priced out of jobs'. The aim of reducing union power was to make the supply side of the economy work better.

Prior would argue that such aims were all very well, but whatever legislation was introduced, it was unlikely to have much effect during the lifetime of a parliament. His presence both as Secretary for Employment until summer 1981 and chairman of the relevant Cabinet sub-committee ensured the carrying out of what had been called his 'softly-softly' approach to union legislation.

Whatever force there was in the argument about the effect of union monopoly on jobs in mid 1979, when unemployment was 1.3 million, it was difficult to sustain the case that it was strengthening during the subsequent four years as unemployment rose towards 3½ million. Yet the 'pricing out of jobs' slogan was to be used repeatedly by the evangelicals throughout this period.

One final point about the run-up to the election, before we plunge into Sir Geoffrey Howe's first important Budget. Just as public feeling was becoming more hostile towards the unions in 1978–79, so much of the financial rectitude shown by Labour in the period 1976–77 was being dissipated. Throughout the winter and spring of 1978–79 Labour knew the election was coming. This, almost inevitably, meant that a lot of difficult decisions were postponed – or taken to the detriment of the 'good housekeeping' on which the Chancellor, Denis Healey, had prided himself in the earlier period.

When Sir Geoffrey and his advisers took their first look at the books after they had won the election, the men who had devoted so much time in opposition study groups to plans for cutting and economizing in public expenditure found that the figures were running well above what had been forecast or revealed. The 'cash limits' discipline had been practised with somewhat less rigour as the election approached: inflation had been higher than expected (the 5 per cent limit had been shattered): and various decisions had been made to give industrial subsidies as the easy way out during the run-up to the election.

Now, as we saw in The Right Approach to the Economy, the Tories had already decided that the direct tax cuts with which they hoped to revitalize British entrepreneurship could not come entirely from expenditure savings, and that indirect taxes would have to be used. What they did not seem prepared for was the sheer scale of the problem when they finally arrived in office. Like many an opposition before them, they prided themselves on the degree to which they had prepared themselves. But when they arrived at No. 10 and the Treasury, they were quite stunned by what they saw. Harold Macmillan had once said, in connection with the difficulty of having sufficient up-to-date information, that running the economy was like trying to catch trains with last year's timetable – or Bradshaw, as it was then known. When the Tories finally received their post-election information, one of the senior economic figures felt they had been conducting the whole campaign, with all its attendant promises, with the previous year's Bradshaw.

The Right Approach to the Economy had contained 'building blocks' to illustrate the trade-off between various possible tax cuts and the public expenditure bill. Some rise in indirect taxes had always been on the cards. What the Tories now found, however, was that there were difficulties they had not dreamed of in their worst nightmares if they were to fulfil their specific election promises about tax cuts and be true to their pledge progressively to reduce the rate of growth of the money supply.

On this latter aim, it is worth recalling that there was a simple formula, which the Labour government and the Bank of England had been using since the inception of monetary targets in 1976, that connected the various financial targets. One of the principal influences on the money supply (M3) was the public sector borrowing requirement. To the extent that the latter was reduced, so was the increase in the money supply. There was thus a neat accounting device or formula which rationalized, in regular policy discussions, those two great aims of the economic evangelicals: less growth in money supply and less public spending. Indeed, success in cutting public expenditure, and therefore having to borrow less, offered the simultaneous additional bonus of cutting monetary growth. (The Bank of England had failed to discover the close connection alleged by the evangelicals between M3 and the subsequent inflation rate; but that was another matter.) But within a few days of assuming occupancy of No. 10 and No. 11 Downing Street, the government was clearly in something of a panic. The figures for the money supply and public sector borrowing (M3 and the infamous initials PSBR which were to be bandied about so much) were much higher than they thought, and – it was forecast – were going to get even worse.

The Tories had scratched around actively in opposition for every potential cut in public spending they could think of. And they had ruled out certain areas for cuts, such as pensions, at least partly with an eye on the election. What is more, the party had made much of its intention to *increase* public spending in certain areas close to its heart, such as external defence and internal law and order (e.g. for higher pay for the police), and an estimate had to be made for the effect of the Clegg awards on cash limits. The figures

presented to them when they arrived gave them a salutary
shock, which brought them down to earth after the euphoria
of the election victory.

Recognizing that the imminence of the election limited his
room for manoeuvre, Denis Healey had introduced a relatively simple Budget in the spring of 1979. After their
election victory, the Tories introduced the 'real' 1979 Budget
within six weeks. Budgets are prepared by the Chancellor
with the aid of a Budget committee, and are largely a
Treasury affair. There are representatives from inside and
outside Whitehall, and the Bank of England is naturally
heavily involved in the monetary side. There is normally
close consultation between the Chancellor and the Prime
Minister on the Budget strategy, and if a Prime Minister is as
strong as Margaret Thatcher, and as interested in the economy as she, then prime-ministerial approval for the Budget
is not necessarily a mere formality. 'There has,' one of her
colleagues said, 'never been a Prime Minister so interested
in the economy or its details.'

The biggest shock to Mrs Thatcher's system during the
preparations for that first Budget was delivered by Sir
Geoffrey Howe on a visit to No. 10. Sir Geoffrey himself was
only just recovering from the shock of receiving it from his
officials. In effect Sir Geoffrey had to say: 'Prime Minister, if
we are to go ahead with our plan to reduce income tax from
33p to 30p we shall have to raise VAT from 8 per cent to 15
per cent.'

The plan to reduce income tax to 30 per cent was itself a
political quid pro quo for a dramatic reduction in the top rate
of income tax, from 83 per cent to 60 per cent. It was the high
top rate which evangelical businessmen had convinced the
Conservatives was the greatest barrier to entrepreneurial
initiative, the release of new energies, and so on. Both the
Prime Minister and Sir Geoffrey felt that if the top rate was
to come down so much, they would be very unpopular if
they merely reduced the standard rate by 1p or 2p. But the
cost of the wider tax concessions was enormous: altogether
the new government, while aiming to reduce the PSBR, was
offering tax reductions of some £4¼ billion a year. Even

plans to cut 3 per cent off the volume of public spending were not enough to counterbalance this. It was in this context that the 15 per cent VAT proposal came up.

Not for the last time in her economic stewardship, Mrs Thatcher found herself trying to square a circle – or, rather, asking her Chancellor to. She wanted the top rate down; she wanted 3p off standard income tax to please the average voter; but she did not want a 15 per cent VAT rate. Sir Geoffrey was despatched back to the Treasury, and told to try again. There he consulted John Biffen, his Chief Secretary, one of the most devout of the evangelicals and the Treasury's 'axe-man' in direct charge of spending cuts. One of the original band of early 1970s monetarists, Biffen was much respected by Mrs Thatcher for his advice, which was always forthright, and not just in private. He belonged to the group who believed British industry needed a shock to the system; since in his view all else had failed, monetarism should at least be tried, he argued (without necessarily having much hope for its success). He also held passionate views about the tax structure, believing that the balance between direct and indirect taxation was all wrong; he felt that the weight of direct taxation was one of the problems of the system, arguing, in common with many advocates in this sphere, that taxing expenditure rather than incomes was an incentive not only to work, but also to save.

Biffen's advice, which was to be decisive in this first Budget, was therefore not based on a desire to minimize the effect of the other elements in the Budget arithmetic on VAT. On the contrary, he wanted a large increase in the tax anyway. What is more, as Treasury officials were to discover to their fascinated irritation, Biffen was less passionate than the rest of his monetarist colleagues in his view on public spending. Whereas he went along with the broad bias of the Tories against the public sector and in favour of the private, he did not take the sort of vehemently hostile attitude towards public spending of, say, Nigel Lawson – who as Financial Secretary was to become heavily involved in the application of the monetarist policy, and who would have liked Biffen to be fiercer. Biffen was much more sympathetic to the public's qualms about cuts in public spending which directly affect them – leading for example to queues in waiting rooms, poorer standards at schools, and cuts in library services. Thus Biffen wanted a big rise in VAT, but was hardly the man to volunteer to be even more severe in wielding the public expenditure axe than he had already been. He was much respected by Mrs Thatcher, and he was the perfect ally for Sir Geoffrey Howe, who wanted to make an immediate impact with the direct tax cuts.

Having held out the hope of a reduction in the standard rate to 25p during the lifetime of the parliament, Howe felt that, after all the fuss the Tories had made during the campaign, they must at least cut the standard rate to 30p in this first Budget. He returned to No. 10 with Biffen, and Biffen delivered a powerful lecture to Mrs Thatcher on the regrets previous administrations had had over not seizing their chances straightaway. He argued that they would find it politically difficult to be so bold later, but in the wake of the election victory they had the public behind them. He ended by saying: 'If you don't do it now you will never be able to do it.'

Biffen's sermon had a powerful impact. The Prime Minister and the Chancellor were now united on the Budget. For all the horror with which the VAT decision would be received by Cabinet, the Chancellor and his Chief Secretary had the Prime Minister's backing. And although Mrs Thatcher's often peremptory and abrasive manner was to cause much unease among Cabinet colleagues and Whitehall officials, there was one area in which her personal manner was highly praised all round: once she had thrown her weight behind a decision, she stuck to her guns, and backed the man who had persuaded her. Indeed, her backing for the Treasury team when the inevitable criticism erupted over the VAT decision misled many into believing at the time that it had been proposed by her, not by Sir Geoffrey Howe and John Biffen.

The work done in opposition on possible public spending cuts – under a group which included Sir Geoffrey, John Nott (who was first Trade Secretary and later at Defence), David

Howell and the political adviser Adam Ridley – was, as we have seen, nowhere near sufficient for the scale of the task the Tories faced when they came into office, if, that is, they were to fulfil their chosen aims. The new government only achieved the scale of the spending cuts they did introduce in their first Budget after a meeting at No. 10 Downing Street where Mrs Thatcher read the riot act to the senior Treasury official on the public expenditure side, Sir Anthony Rawlinson. And, as we have seen, the minister in charge of public spending cuts, John Biffen, did not have his heart in all of them.

One of the most curious aspects of the June 1979 Budget, however, concerns the *raison d'être* for the whole thing – namely the alleged incentive effects of the large tax cuts. The Conservatives had managed to convince themselves that the tax burden in the UK was particularly crippling, whereas comparative statistics from the Paris-based Organization for Economic Cooperation and Development indicated that it was about average. While it was acknowledged that marginal tax rates were unusually high at the top end of the scale, it was no secret that many in this bracket had so arranged their affairs that their actual payments were much lower. But even without this, the Conservatives were placing a touching amount of faith in the argument that miracles of entrepreneurial initiative would arise from lower tax rates. One is reminded of the Michael Frayn character who says: 'You mean I can get more money for the same amount of work? Yes, sure I'll work harder.' And, as we shall see, the macro-economic climate in which to exercise any new-found entrepreneurial freedoms was going to get progressively harsher.

Again, the alleged incentive effects which lay behind the huge rise in VAT were also open to debate. What the combination of lower direct taxes and higher indirect taxes essentially boils down to is giving with one hand and taking away with the other. The incentive effects of such devices were questionable to say the least. Much more tangible from the beginning, however, were the risks and disadvantages of the VAT increase. Whatever the arguments about the effects on 'incentives' of a switch from direct to indirect taxation, the rise in VAT in the June 1979 Budget was a major strategic error in the context of the battle against inflation, which the Tories had identified as the *sine qua non* before their hopes for reviving the economy could be realized.

The VAT increase itself automatically added nearly four percentage points to the retail price index – the principal and most widely quoted inflation index, and the one almost universally consulted by both unions and employers in wage negotiations. At the same time, as part of their general philosophy of attempting to make the nationalized industries pay their way, the Tories removed some of the subsidies that Labour had given them. The result of this and the VAT decision together was to add nearly six percentage points to the RPI. The Chancellor and Chief Secretary were fully warned at the time by senior Treasury officials of the implications of what they were doing. Those warnings proved all too well founded. The rise in VAT, as just mentioned, had a swift impact on the RPI and seriously worsened the pay bargaining climate, which was in any case poor on account of the Clegg 'give them the money' pay award to the public sector.

What the Budget did achieve was a sharp impact on those objectives regarding inflation which were at the heart of the analysis contained in *The Right Approach to the Economy*: the only trouble was that the impact was entirely in the wrong direction. It is difficult to conceive of how any government could have so allowed inflationary expectations to alter for the worse, in such a short time, while professing to want to do the opposite.

What were the possible excuses for this? Those closest to the decision have tended to rationalize it with the argument that Labour would have done something similar anyway. This is a reference to the options – including a rise in VAT – that had been presented to Denis Healey as means of adhering to relatively tight public sector borrowing targets. But this takes us into the barren area of what might have happened. It is certainly a curious line of justification to introduce a revolutionary tax change and, when it is criticized, to argue that 'The Opposition would have done it anyway'.

The best way to interpret the decision is that, under the influence of Biffen, the government did seize the only opportunity they would have to make such a revolutionary alteration to the tax structure – i.e. the first Budget – but that that decision, politically brave though it might have been, was in direct conflict with the much greater good of reducing inflation and inflationary expectations. One way of looking at it is to note that, in one Budget alone, the new government added the equivalent of a whole year's inflation in Germany to the retail prices index.

The decision is an outstanding illustration of an aspect of the approach to government by the Thatcher administration which, ironically, one arm of it was doing its utmost to avoid. John Hoskyns, at the No. 10 policy unit, brought to the government a concern with what he called 'hierarchies' – an attempt to distinguish the major from the minor issues. Manifestos are essentially lists of promises, and sometimes these promises are in direct conflict with one another. Reducing the balance between direct and indirect taxation was in conflict with reducing inflationary expectations because of the impact first on the RPI and second on wage demands.

When an erroneous decision has been taken, it is a natural human reaction to resort to an attempt to rationalize it. One way was to say, 'Healey would have done it anyway' (although Healey was within weeks of losing office to start writing newspaper articles attacking the obsession with the PSBR which led to such tax balancing acts). Another, more interesting and significant rationalization, conveniently served up by some of the monetarists with whom the party was so much in love, was the argument that the impact of the decision would not be inflationary at all.

Here we come to probably the most naive aspect of the Thatcher experiment. As we have seen earlier, monetarists preached that inflation could only be caused by increases in the money supply. Despite the overridingly strong connection in Britain between the RPI and wage inflation, some of those closest to the Prime Minister argued in the summer of 1979 that, provided the money supply was properly controlled, then the Budget need not be inflationary in its impact *at all*. It was such rationalizations that caused one to begin to understand how much politicians had seized upon, or resorted to, monetarism as a kind of magic potion, which charmed away all the practical problems.

After the inflationary explosion which followed the 1979 Budget, it is not surprising that there is a tendency on the part of ministers to say with hindsight that they never believed in the monetarist solution at the time. They all agree that it was essential to appear to believe in it, in order to influence inflationary expectations (in the opposite way to which they were actually being influenced). But such arguments do not really wash; they certainly did not wash at the time; and it is my strong belief, based on the public statements and private conversations of ministers at the time, that the monetarists believed the inflationary impact of the Budget could and would be offset by some magical monetary means whose mechanism they were quite unable to explain.

In pure theory this was perfectly valid. But the argument – or hope – begged important questions both about the mechanism of inflationary forces in the UK and the mechanism of monetary control. And when the figures showed that things were not working out in accordance with the theories of naive monetarism, the critical attitude of ministers was inevitably going to focus on the messenger – in this case the Bank of England.

Which brings us to one of the oddest aspects of all in our present examination: the quite remarkable lack of preparation on the part of the Tories in opposition for what was going to become the focal point of their economic policies – namely their monetarism. We have noted how Keith Joseph and others became monetarists; and we have also seen how the ideas of Milton Friedman were promulgated in the British press. But the curious thing is that, although the Tories in opposition spent a lot of time on drawing up lists of possible cuts in public expenditure, and although they agonized over the perennial no-man's-land topic of trade union reform, monetary policy received little consideration.

How did this curious state of affairs come about – or, rather, not come about? One important point was that, although Milton Friedman himself made great claims for monetarism as such, he had no particular pretensions about his knowledge of the British economy, the British financial system, or the British Central Bank. And his disciples, or those who care to be known as his disciples, were scattered, not always in agreement, and not necessarily very knowledgeable about the practicalities of what they were preaching. Their argument tended to be: 'Excessive monetary growth causes inflation and you must therefore control the money supply.' How the money supply was to be controlled; what exactly was to be controlled; and how the demand for money fitted in with the supply of money . . . these were questions that were far from exhaustively examined. 'We shall control inflation by controlling inflation' tautologically summarized the general intention.

There had been three formal study groups while the Conservatives were in opposition, covering pay and the unions, public expenditure, and fiscal measures. This was deliberate policy on the part of the moderates, or wets, who still exercised more control in the years 1975–79 over formal discussions than Mrs Thatcher and Sir Keith Joseph would have liked. As one moderate put it: 'We knew the monetarists were loonies, each with his separate obsession – narrow definitions of money, wide definitions of money, weekly money supply figures, daily money supply figures . . .'

The moderates' influence on the study groups in opposition misled them into not taking monetarism too seriously. 'We were helped in ignoring them by the fact that the more rabid monetarists were notable by their absence' – a reference to the fact that Alan Walters was then working in the US and David Laidler in Canada. Nevertheless, both Mrs Thatcher and Sir Keith Joseph had individually managed to have a number of sessions with economists of varying degrees of monetarist leanings during their opposition years. Mrs Thatcher's teachers included Professor Patrick Minford of

Liverpool University, Professor Brian Griffiths of the London School of Economics and the City University, Professor Harold Rose of Barclays Bank, Mr Gordon Pepper of stock-brokers W. Greenwell, and Mr John Sparrow of the merchant bank Morgan Grenfell (who subsequently became head of the Think Tank when Sir Kenneth Berrill retired).

Perhaps inevitably, this private and somewhat unstructured approach to the mastering of the economic faith they had espoused left the monetarist politicians somewhat confused when they arrived in office. The differences of approach, emphasis and belief of their various academic advisers did not help either, not least when it came to consultations on the June 1979 Budget. Every monetarist approached by the Tories tended to give a different version of how things worked and how he would go about applying the cure. Thus some – e.g. Patrick Minford of Liverpool University – argued that the VAT decision did not matter at all, while others – e.g. the London Business School – showed more concern about the impact of the VAT decision. In so far as the Treasury and Bank of England raised objections, and offered unpalatable forecasts, there was a strong inclination on the part of the monetarists to dismiss them. Were these not the men who had got the economy into the state the Tories had inherited? Was it not precisely this sort of pessimism and raising of difficulties on the part of the bureaucracy that had to be changed? If the VAT increase was fed into the inflation figures, was it not obvious that the Bank of England was failing to do its job properly? And if the official forecasts showed that inflation would rise sharply, was there not something wrong with the official forecasts?

Such thoughts, doubts, rationalizations were very much in evidence at the time. One monetarist academic would say to ministers, 'The rise in VAT is not inflationary; provided the money supply is not expanded, everything will be all right.' Another would say, in connection with the Clegg public sector wage awards, 'Wages don't cause inflation,' and ministers would take refuge in this dubious haven too.

It was not just in the VAT decision that one entry on the manifesto list (one of the most important ones: lowering inflationary expectations) came into conflict with another: redressing the balance between direct and indirect taxation. As we have seen, the Clegg awards – honouring a campaign promise – also contradicted the more basic anti-inflation strategy. The public sector awards duly influenced the wage bargaining climate in the private sector. And in this whole area of wage bargaining, there was yet another contradiction in the application of manifesto promises: once again, the great aim of reducing inflation proved incompatible with the desire to restore 'responsible collective bargaining'.

Yet again, there had been study groups working in opposition on the need to reduce the size of the nationalized sector, and to make the rump which could not be returned to the private sector at least more responsive to the pressure of market forces. Denationalization, or privatization, was to take time – and not necessarily to rank very high in those Hoskyns 'hierarchies'. But a great dash was made early to attempt to restore market discipline to the public sector. In the run-up to the election, one of Labour's quasi-electioneering tactics had been to subsidize nationalized industry and public corporation prices, and /or to allow them to delay price increases as long as possible. The Tories wanted to put an end to this, not only in accordance with their traditional thinking in these matters, but also because of their desperate desire to find savings in public expenditure wherever they could.

There was nothing particularly monetarist or unduly right-wing about this aim. But the result of the sudden change, and of the freedom given to the nationalized industries, was to add a further 2½ percentage points to the Retail Prices Index on top of the VAT decision. This probably received much less attention than the VAT decision with regard to its impact on the RPI and wage-inflationary climate of 1979 – although rumblings about the behaviour of the nationalized industries and government's attitude to them were to get louder as time went on. There was thus the direct impact on the RPI – which affected *all* wage negotiations that year – and the impact of Clegg, plus the removal of price restraint on nationalized industries in starting a wage–price spiral in the nationalized sector itself; and the rise in nationalized industry charges was to cause increasing complaints from the private sector of industry in the following years.

This quite remarkable rise in the RPI during the summer of 1979 – the 'year on year' figure rose from 10.3 per cent in May to 16.5 per cent in September, and thence to 21.9 per cent in May 1980 – was not exactly taking place against a background of subdued economic activity, which might have been conducive to dampening the inflationary climate. Production and retail sales were expanding quite fast. The breakdown of Labour's incomes policy had produced one of Britain's periodic bouts of 'free for all' wage bargaining. And the Tories added all these inflationary impulses on top.

In the face of all these factors, they went ahead with a Budget aimed at slowing down the economy, and at being counter-inflationary in monetarist terms. The forecasts presented to them showed that the monetary expansion in the economy was such that, in order to offset part of it by attracting savings and selling more government stock, they would have to raise interest rates. Raising interest rates is the classic method for the Bank of England to sell more government stock; once the financial markets become convinced that interest rates have reached a peak from which they are more likely to fall than not, then there are capital gains to be made by buying government stock immediately. Much to their chagrin, then, the new government found themselves having to raise interest rates by 2 per cent in the June Budget, in order to improve the outlook for monetary growth. This in turn was meant to improve the outlook for inflation.

Here, once again, there was endless scope for confusion and rationalization about the likely course of inflation. On one interpretation, if the growth of money supply was held to 9 per cent during the following twelve months, then VAT-induced inflation could simply not occur by definition. On another interpretation, there was a time lag of up to two years between changes in the money supply and subsequent changes in the inflation rate. Either way, the importance of the monetarist path to which ministers stuck at the time was that it gave them a pretext for ignoring the implications of what was staring them in the face – namely the second worst inflationary explosion in Britain since the war. Their policies, if they did not actually ignite, certainly added fuel to a fire they had been elected to put out.

It was of course open to the Tories when they got in – at least in theory – to cite the seriousness of the situation, the poor condition of the inheritance, as a reason for changing their minds, for going slow. What prevented them was, first, the euphoria and political momentum of winning the election with a comfortable working majority: this fired their enthusiasm for going ahead with the tax cuts; second, a philosophical repugnance for dealing with the inflationary crisis with methods they had spent five years reacting against, such as incomes policy, or a sharp freeze to damp down inflationary expectation; third, there was no sign of an old-style foreign exchange market crisis to force them into changing their minds about these first two factors. That was to come later, and to prove a quite different sort of foreign exchange market crisis from what Britain had been accustomed to since the war.

If there were two possible routes for monetarism to work – the soft way of reducing inflationary expectations and the hard way of deflating the economy until it hurt – then the 1979 Budget certainly ruled out the soft way. Inflationary expectations were drastically increased, not reduced.

Treasury officials duly tried to voice their doubts. The increases in wages and costs implied by the VAT rise, the implementation of Clegg pay awards, and the sudden freeing of nationalized industry prices all meant that there would be an increase in the demand for money to finance ordinary business transactions. This presaged extraordinary tension for any given increase in the money supply. But the evangelical ministers actually demanded that the targets for money supply, in spite of the worsening outlook for inflation, should be tightened – from a range of 8 to 12 per cent inherited from Denis Healey to the more precise figure of 9 per cent.

The worst of all worlds was now in prospect: failure to meet the incredibly tight monetary targets; higher and higher interest rates in an attempt to choke off the extra demand for money; and higher unemployment if the attempt to meet the targets was to be persisted with.

Within their own monetarist framework the government were projecting a very tight economic squeeze. They were making it extraordinarily difficult for themselves to achieve the target they had set their hearts on. Given the way the inflation figures were now moving, most conventional economists probably expected some disinflationary action, not least those members of the Keynesian economic establishment who had lost their faith in the efficacy of incomes policies after the winter of 1978–79. But deliberately putting more inflationary pressures in the pipeline before one embarked on the disinflationary route . . .

This was a new administration, with a clear majority. It had firm economic goals, and thought it knew how to achieve them. But even many monetarists had to resort to sophistry to argue that the 1979 Budget was not inflationary – on lines such as 'It will simply alter the *profile* of inflation, in that in the long run (five years?) the unemployment resulting from the monetary squeeze will eventually bring down costs.' But ministers such as John Biffen, John Nott, and especially Nigel Lawson, the energetic and forceful Financial Secretary to the Treasury, were repeatedly to be heard inside and outside Whitehall saying that wages did not cause inflation and the money supply would be controlled. And there was to be many a meeting from now on when Sir Douglas Wass, the Permanent Secretary to the Treasury, would speak on the following lines: 'Sitting in these uncomfortable clothes, this is no doubt what you will be wanting to do, Chancellor . . .'

CHAPTER FIVE

1980 TO 1983

Four Deflationary Years

I have deliberately placed Sir Geoffrey Howe's first Budget in the context of the Conservatives' preparations for office, for one simple reason: the tax cuts were essentially a political gesture, introduced in the heat of electoral success. From an economic policy point of view, the government were from now on having to struggle not only against the familiar trends of the British economy and the exacerbation caused by the 'inheritance', but also against the limitations posed by the manifesto itself and by their own first Budget. For, as was to become increasingly apparent, that first Budget was not to be interpreted as part of their broader economic strategy, but as a hindrance to it.

A major theme of the next three years from June 1979 was to be the economic and political price the government risked in order to bring the rate of inflation back to the sort of level that had been inherited. The economic price was to be manifested in a fall in output on a scale not experienced since the 1920s, and a concomitant rise in unemployment. Some of this would have happened anyway, as a result of the general recession sparked off by the recrudescence of the energy problem and deepened by the adoption of restrictive economic policies around the world. But the British economy was to suffer more than most – as seen, for example, by the fact that unemployment rose to 3 million in Britain by mid 1982, compared with 2 million in France and Germany, and that by January 1983 the UK unemployment rate was 13.3 per cent (7.8 percentage points higher than in 1979) compared with the OECD countries' average of 8.9 per cent (3.8 percentage points higher than in 1979).

I have found virtually no evidence that the Tories either wanted or expected unemployment to rise to such heights. I will argue that a significant part of the differences between the rise in unemployment in Britain and abroad during these three years was the result of their policies. But the policies worked in two ways, direct and indirect. For instance, the monetarist clique made no bones about the consequences for unemployment if unions insisted on pricing themselves out of jobs. Monetarism, or fiscal conservatism, certainly implied higher unemployment (that was at the heart of Sir Keith Joseph's original analysis). But an important part of my analysis is that the monetarist ideology, and in particular its rigid interpretation in terms of M3 and the alleged link with inflation, meant that warning signals in the economy were not heeded, and sensible reactions were delayed.

The entrenchment of the ideology was assisted by the Prime Minister's decision to keep economic policy very much in the hands of the monetarist clique. They, in turn, were to strengthen their defences by a succession of misleading claims that things were not as bad as all that, and, from the winter of 1981, statements on the lines of 'recovery is just around the corner'. And when the objections of so-called 'wet' opponents in the Cabinet began to grow, various expedients were open to the monetarists. One was the time-honoured resort of sacking the critics. Another was that of hitting back – so that, for example, if the wets won a battle over public expenditure cuts, the Chancellor could come back with other devices – the 'medium term financial strategy' in the Budget of 1980, and the unexpected tax increases in the Budget of 1981 – which rendered the wets' victory less significant, in terms of the overall stance of fiscal policy, than was generally appreciated (an echo of what Denis Healey did to the Labour Cabinet in 1976).

I have argued in a previous book[1] that British economic policy tends to be controlled by a tightly knit group. The Treasury is the pre-eminent economic department and, as head of the Treasury, the Chancellor of the Exchequer exercises considerable sway. The Bank of England, which has to conduct the government's monetary and exchange rate policies in the field, is also very closely involved in key economic decisions. During the period of the late 1970s, when monetary policy came to the fore, the Bank's influence was seen to increase.

If a crucial decision has to be taken about interest rates or the exchange rate, then the Bank of England – as the government's agent in the market place – will naturally be closely involved. In such central areas as budgetary policy and taxation decisions, the Bank plays an indirect role, pointing out the likely effects on the PSBR and the money supply of any particular budgetary proposal; these considerations may in turn have implications for interest rates and the exchange rate which bring the Bank into the centre of policy.

Since the economy is at the forefront of so much of public debate in Britain, the Prime Minister, too, tends to be heavily involved in economic strategy. As a general rule, a Prime Minister has so many other responsibilities that traditionally he tends to flit in and out of the economic policy arena. Mrs Thatcher, by contrast, was to give many people the impression she never left it. Although much of the detailed preparation was done elsewhere, the crucial strategic decisions on economic policy under the first Thatcher administration were taken at meetings at No. 10 Downing Street. (Many a detailed discussion took place there, too. A senior official commented: 'I should be thinking about major policy issues before I go to No. 10. But what I really have to concentrate on is not being caught out over what the local authority borrowing figure was in the quarter before last.')

This heavy prime-ministerial involvement was intrinsic to the nature of the Thatcher economic experiment. The economic evangelicals had very specific ends in view, and had willed very specific means. The narrowness of these means – the restricted focus on M3 and the PSBR – was alien to the traditional eclecticism of the economic policy machine, which, dominated by the Treasury, liked to pull every possible lever of policy in the difficult job of trying to run the British economy.

While Treasury officials may have gone to great lengths to make allowances for, in what were reportedly Sir Douglas Wass's words, the 'uncomfortable clothes' worn by the government's economic ministers, it was natural that such a determined Prime Minister should be disinclined to trust them too far. This applied *a fortiori* to a Prime Minister who was on many occasions to make a virtue of showing contempt for the Civil Service as such – a contempt which she found perfectly compatible with great liking and trust for certain individual officials. Indeed, the new administration's regular assaults on the Civil Service prompted one official to observe: 'Bashing the Civil Service is the other half of what the Thatcher experiment is about' (the first half being 'bashing the trade unions').

Prime-ministerial involvement in economic policy was going to be strong under Mrs Thatcher's administration. As we have seen, her very rise to power in the Conservative Party had been in the wake of Sir Keith Joseph's disavowal of previous Conservative measures. The mixture of monetarism and right-wing economics suited her own populist approach, which was characterized by a vague but strongly expressed belief in freedom and old-fashioned values – one of which was good housekeeping.

Hugh Stephenson in his book[2] compared the role of Sir Geoffrey Howe vis-à-vis Mrs Thatcher to that of the good country solicitor doing his best for an important client. Many others close to Howe have likened him to a barrister sticking doggedly to his brief. Mrs Thatcher's legal training is also often cited as an explanation of how she entered No. 10 determined to fight the battle for economic evangelicalism to the end. Such analogies have their value, but can be misleading. There have been plenty of lawyers in politics who have taken a more flexible and pragmatic approach to policy, and been prepared, as it were, to change their briefs when the occasion suited. Perhaps the most important point about Mrs Thatcher was the impression she gave of sheer determination and strength of personality – on account of which, in the context of foreign affairs, she had already been christened 'the Iron Lady'. Later, in the run-up to the 1983 election, she was credited with the 'resolute approach'. (As is not unknown with such personalities, this public determination co-existed with private spells of doubt and indecision. One observer commented: 'At heart this determined woman is deeply insecure.')

This public show of determination was seen in the way she used that great prime-ministerial prerogative – choice of Cabinet committees and organization of Cabinet business – to keep control of economic policy-making. Simon Hoggart has pointed out[3] that Mrs Thatcher was surprisingly ill-prepared for office and had no firm ideas about the composition of her Cabinet. She relied on the man she had defeated in the contest for the leadership – the deputy leader, Willie Whitelaw – for advice on some key appointments, and the first Cabinet contained a fair proportion of the sort of moderates who were subsequently to be designated 'wets'. Another, not impossible, interpretation could be that knowing her own rise to power was a kind of accident, she initially tried to strengthen her base (and reduce her sense of insecurity). At all events, she was well-nigh conventional in her choice of the Cabinet as a whole, in which the traditional centre of the party was well represented by Lord Carrington, Lord Hailsham, Lord Soames, William Whitelaw and Francis Pym. As her strength and confidence grew, the balance was going to change. Although there was nothing resembling Macmillan's Night of the Long Knives, by the end of her third year of office a quarter of the original Cabinet had been replaced.

But the relatively conventional nature of the Cabinet was deceptive from the point of view of economic policy, for she gave the economic appointments – other than the Department of Employment – to people who, at least at that stage, belonged to the economic evangelical movement. Geoffrey Howe, for instance, was not just a lawyer carrying out a brief: he believed in what he described as a 'Welsh fundamentalist' way that public sector borrowing should be progressively cut. John Nott, at the Department of Trade to begin with, before his adventures in the Falklands Islands as Minister of Defence, was a passionate enthusiast of the monetarist cause.

Sir Keith Joseph, who was given command of the Department of Industry, was, of course, the Prime Minister's mentor. And other members of the faithful to play important roles in the Treasury were John Biffen, as Chief Secretary, and Nigel Lawson, as Financial Secretary.

During 1979, Mrs Thatcher prevented the full Cabinet from discussing economic strategy at all. This was left to 'E' (for economy) committee, which, although it contained James Prior and Peter Walker (a former Industry and Environment Secretary, now given the almost part-time job of Agriculture Minister), was effectively packed with monetarist sympathizers. Long-term economic strategy was in the hands of a small new economic sub-committee dominated by Howe and Joseph, which also contained John Hoskyns (who had, as we have seen, strong views on the need to redress the balance of economic power within Britain) and Sir Kenneth Berrill, head of the Think Tank. (Berrill, although previously considered by many to be an old-fashioned Keynesian, had by this time become disillusioned with the unions, and had arrived at the conclusion that something had to be done about the power of organized labour in the country.)

There were three individuals to watch with particular interest as the policy unfolded. They were the Prime Minister, who was to prove strangely erratic, wanting to stick to the main purpose, but allowing the politician in her to object to the means she had willed – such as cuts in certain areas of public spending, or rises in mortgage interest rates; Sir Geoffrey Howe himself, who was going to bat on the monetarist wicket with all the doggedness of one of those slow-scoring batsmen such as Trevor Bailey or Willie Watson in the England cricket team of the 1950s; and Nigel Lawson, who, in the words of one Treasury official, 'just took this place by storm. Whatever we thought of his ideas, we had to admire his intellect and his tenacity. He was a really effective minister, making the Financial Secretary's role into an unusually important one.' (In doing so, of course, Lawson was laying down his marker for the job of Chancellor in Mrs Thatcher's second administration.)

The forcefulness of ministers such as Lawson and the

Prime Minister herself was an outstanding characteristic of the Thatcher economic administration. Previous administrations, both Conservative and Labour, had come into office with strong manifesto commitments, and found themselves being driven off course at one stage or another: there had been the Heath U-turn of 1971–72, and the Wilson / Callaghan administration's resort to the International Monetary Fund in 1976. The distinguishing feature of the first Thatcher administration was its strong reaction against such precedents: indeed, distaste for them had helped to give birth to, and was a fundamental part of, its ideology.

Once the June 1979 Budget was out of the way, the economic debate tended to be dominated in both Cabinet and the press by the government's public spending plans. Much preparatory work had been done on possible areas for cuts, but of course the state of the books when the government assumed office made the public spending problem look even more intractable than expected. Moreover, during the rest of 1979 both the effects of the Clegg pay awards on public spending and the impact of higher interest charges on the cost of the government's debt servicing were to make the problem look even worse. Once again, the 'inheritance' problem was partly of the government's own making, not only because of Clegg, but also because the Tories had promised to increase public expenditure on defence and law and order, and had promised to protect the health service and the real value of pensions.

In looking for public spending cuts during July 1979 – to take effect in the subsequent financial year 1980–81 – the Treasury ministers started with the aim of £8,000 million and ended up, after stiff Cabinet and departmental resistance, with £3,500 million. As the year went on, the problem looked worse, and the winter months saw bitter fights in Cabinet as the Treasury ministers sought another £1,000 million of cuts for 1980–81, and a further £2,000 million off the programme for subsequent years.

It was clear from the start – from the manifesto commitments, in fact – that the wilder ideas for cutting public spending put forward by the economic evangelicals of the

Institute of Economic Affairs and the Centre for Policy Studies were not on. There was, for example, a fundamental belief on the part of the bulk of the Conservative Party, including Mrs Thatcher, that the British public liked a free health service, but wanted it to work better. Fanciful schemes for issuing educational vouchers were seen to be prohibitively expensive if the poorest were to be given the freedom of choice that proponents of vouchers said they believed in. On the other hand, it was felt that savings could be made through cutbacks in public sector housing, which would basically be in tune with the belief that the electorate's bias was in favour of private housing anyway – Eden's famous 'property-owning democracy'. (Selling council houses was to prove a great electoral success.)

The November 1979 White Paper 'The Government's Expenditure Plans 1980–81' restated the philosophy we have traced earlier, and linked the public spending objectives with the government's monetarism. 'Public expenditure is at the heart of Britain's present economic difficulties,' it stated. The government would plan for spending levels compatible with its objectives on borrowing and taxation – taxation objectives being determined by the need to restore 'incentives', borrowing by the need to lower the rate of inflation by reducing the growth of the money supply (to which borrowing contributed, although, as Professor Nicholas Kaldor has pointed out,[4] by far the greatest component of the increase in M3 during the 1970s was not the PSBR but the growth of bank lending).

Another strand, often referred to by Treasury ministers and a favourite theme of the Prime Minister at this time, was the need to reduce the size of the public sector in order to 'create room' for the expansion of the private sector. This argument was sometimes put in terms of the need to prevent the public sector from 'crowding out' the private sector. (The concept of 'crowding out' may have been relevant to a fully employed and fast-growing economy, but not to the recession which was to develop in 1980 and 1981.)

The government achieved the difficult feat of displeasing nearly all its adherents with the three cuts exercises aimed at in 1980–81. The centre and left of the Cabinet were so upset that as early as February 1980 Sir Ian Gilmour began the series of public criticisms that were eventually to cost him his Cabinet job – at first he spoke almost in code, about the true nature of Conservatism. The monetarists were dissatisfied with what they regarded as their limited success in winning expenditure cuts; the wets with the fact that the cuts were beginning to impinge on the real value of child benefit payments – on which the then Social Services Secretary, Patrick Jenkin, had made several commitments to the contrary – and on unemployment and sickness benefits (which were taxed from 1982, and from which the earnings-related supplement was removed). From November 1979 to the end of January 1980 there was bitter wrangling in and around Cabinet about these cuts. The Prime Minister's and Treasury team's determination had only been increased by the fact that in November, in order to reactivate the gilt-edged market and slow down (they hoped) the demand for bank advances and the growth of money supply, they had raised the Minimum Lending Rate to a record 17 per cent. Raising interest rates was repugnant even to politicians whose monetarist theories indicated that this was necessary. The move was pressed on them by the Bank of England and Treasury officials, in a purely traditional response to the paralysis of the gilt market; this reflected worries about the PSBR, which was itself being swollen by the impact of the Clegg awards.

There were already signs of a vicious circle developing. The November 1979 economic forecasts showed that output in the economy was expected to fall by 3 per cent in 1980; unemployment to rise to 2 million by 1981; and the corporate sector's profits and financial position were likely to deteriorate sharply. The traditional reaction of the economic establishment would have been to say that, in a recession, higher public sector borrowing was a natural event – inevitable as tax receipts fell and unemployment disbursements rose – and an automatic stabilizer of the economy.

This was also thought to be the belief at the time of the new Chief Economic Adviser chosen by the Treasury in autumn 1979 – Terry Burns, from the London Business School. Geoffrey Howe and Nigel Lawson, however, felt so passionately about reducing the PSBR that they fought this point. Lawson even took issue with the forecasts, saying he did not believe them and they did not take enough account of the incentive effects of the government's policy. (The theoretical position of these hardliners later softened a little, so that the principle of a cyclically adjusted PSBR was conceded – in small print. But the practical bias remained, as events were to demonstrate.)

Burns joined the Treasury as Chief Economic Adviser at the beginning of January 1980, but was in close touch during the closing months of 1979, after his appointment had been announced in the autumn. He was attractive to the government not only because he was a monetarist, but also because he was a vociferous critic of the traditional policies of devaluation. Burns and the LBS were vigorous proponents of a strong exchange rate, and believed in the virtuous circle of a strong pound leading to lower wage demands, and lower costs, leading to even lower inflation and an even stronger currency. As members of the 'soft' monetarist school, they believed that, through influencing wage bargainers' 'expectations', these aims could be achieved at a minimal cost in output and employment. They also wanted the government's commitment to a monetary attack on inflation to be mapped out over several years, so that it would not be just a passing phase. If monetarism was going to be applied, it had to be applied properly. And if expectations were to be influenced, then people had to be persuaded that the government would not change course.

Burns was one of several monetarist candidates for the Chief Economic Adviser post. He was the most appealing to the Treasury partly because he had built up a reputation as a more eclectic economist than some of the other monetarist candidates – the LBS published widely quoted and respected economic forecasts – and partly, if one was being sceptical about monetarists in general, because he was considered 'sounder' than most of the others. In particular, senior Treasury men thought he shared their belief that the Public

Sector Borrowing Requirement should be allowed to rise during a recession, to reflect the automatic impact of lower tax revenues and higher disbursements on such items as unemployment benefit. There was nothing unusual about this belief among conventional economists. But reduction of the PSBR, come what may, was rapidly becoming the central tenet of the new breed of Tory economic ministers.

Burns was horrified to learn of the size of the 'Clegg effect' when he first received the official government forecasts. These public sector pay awards were pushing up the estimates both of inflation and the PSBR. For a time there was an atmosphere of unreality – almost of 'not wanting to know' – reminiscent of the phase in 1974–75 when the threshold payment awards were pushing up the inflation figures under Labour. Forecasts and estimates were being discussed inside Whitehall 'ex-Clegg' – on the grounds that the impact of the Clegg awards could not yet be properly quantified. All the time wage inflation was racing away, although ministers close to Mrs Thatcher continued to delude themselves – and tried to delude others – into believing that wages had nothing to do with inflation, which was entirely a matter of controlling the money supply. As late as July 1980 the Chief Secretary, John Biffen, was making speeches on these lines.

With the arrival of Burns, the Tories thus for the first time had a monetarist Chief Economic Adviser. Burns was on record as wanting a medium-term monetary plan for the progressive reduction of the inflation rate. And he believed in a causal correlation between changes in the money supply – M3 – and subsequent changes in the inflation rate.*

Such a plan was also being urged by the sympathetic monetarist commentator Samuel Brittan in the *Financial Times*. It was opposed by the Bank of England, which, although it had made the running in the introduction of

---

* His colleague Alan Budd of the LBS was to admit to a meeting of the Society of Business Economists in December 1981 that the 'soft' monetarists had been much too optimistic, particularly in regard to the virtues of a high exchange rate. Burns, too, went a long way towards conceding that they had got their figures wrong at a similar meeting of the SBE in 1982. But this did not seem to shake their faith in monetarism as such.

annual monetary targets, was much too pragmatic in its approach to want to be committed several years ahead – and had already seen in practice how difficult it was to achieve annual targets. The Governor told the Prime Minister that a medium-term monetary plan would be a rod for her own back. John Biffen, so influential in the earlier VAT decision, regarded the idea of a medium-term monetary plan as 'dangerous futurology'. The Chancellor, Sir Geoffrey Howe, was said on this matter, as on many others, to be undecided. Ironically Sir Douglas Wass, the head of the Treasury, who had had a difficult early relationship with the evangelicals, was now leaning over backwards not to offend his political masters, and was unexpectedly receptive towards the scheme.

But Burns's proposal in itself was still not enough to convince a sceptical Treasury. It required ministerial support, and received it from the energetic Financial Secretary, Nigel Lawson. 'Without Lawson,' said one Treasury official, 'the medium-term financial plan would never have got off the ground.'

The medium-term financial plan evolved into the Medium Term Financial Strategy or MTFS. The MTFS was the centrepiece of the Budget in March 1980, although this did not seem to be widely appreciated at the time, and it set out the core of the government's economic strategy for the rest of the Parliament. The only concession to the criticism of the Governor and others was that the targets for monetary growth were now given in ranges: 7 to 11 per cent, 6 to 10 per cent, 5 to 9 per cent, and 4 to 8 per cent for the financial years 1980–81, 1981–82, 1982–83, and 1983–84, instead of the firm figures of 8 per cent, 7 per cent, and 6 per cent originally proposed by Lawson.

The MTFS was the apotheosis both of the intentions of the monetarist clique in opposition and of their determination in that first year of office. It was also a riposte to the wets for their opposition to the public spending cuts proposed by the Chief Secretary. Despite the public ridicule the MTFS was subjected to when monetary statistics went awry, the government was going to stick closely to the core of the plan – which was essentially deflationary. (We had come a long way from the 1960s, when the National Plan was a plan for expansion.)

The MTFS was outlined in the Financial Statement and Budget Report of March 1980. The beauty of the MTFS was that it linked the government's principal political aims with its economic philosophy, and offered light at the end of the tunnel if all went well. The rate of growth of the money supply (M3) was to be progressively reduced over the following four financial years, thereby bringing inflation down to a tolerable rate. A major element in this reduction would be the progressive lowering of the public sector borrowing requirement (PSBR) – itself the result of the plans for a lower volume of public spending outlined in the government's accompanying Public Expenditure White Paper. If all went well, then the final fiscal year 1983–84 – presumably the pre-election period – would allow, according to the tables, a 'fiscal adjustment' – i.e. tax cuts. (Some tax cuts duly came in the pre-election Budget of March 1983; but the recession, and a significant increase in the average tax burden, came first.)

According to the monetary purists who were the most enthusiastic proponents of the scheme, the MTFS offered businessmen a stable environment in which they could plan ahead. Unlike previous administrations, this one would not be diverted from its course, and could be relied upon to make the necessary adjustments to get the economy back on course: for example, if the monetary or borrowing statistics started racing away, then policy would be adjusted accordingly. There would be no let-up in the fight against inflation.

The press seized on the 'fiscal adjustment' story, somewhat to the annoyance of Lawson, the political architect of the MTFS; he felt this diverted attention from the main point, which was to move away from the world where people were always looking to the government to bail them out – e.g. with tax cuts – and to concentrate attention on the virtues of fiscal and monetary discipline.

It so happened that the press was not alone in picking up this aspect. Indeed, the principal reason why the MTFS gained prime-ministerial approval in the pre-Budget meetings at No. 10 was precisely that it did seem to offer light at the end of the tunnel: for the conventional forecasts of output, employment, and inflation were grim. Yet the conventional forecasts, though much distrusted by Lawson and Howe, were the best guide the government had to future developments; for the MTFS, and the fiscal adjustment, were not a forecast, merely a plan. 'The thing about the MTFS was that it was not a strategy at all, merely a statement of objectives,' said one insider. 'There was no real clue as to how we were to get there – because we didn't know.'

Lawson's drive was certainly important in getting the MTFS through initial Treasury scepticism. Given what was happening to the inflation figures, the Treasury was in a mood to try almost anything. 'I don't necessarily think the emphasis on monetary policy was a mistake, or even the MTFS,' said one official. 'But I do think setting up conditions in which it couldn't work was a mistake.' This was a reference to the strains imposed from the start on the MTFS, which was after all aimed at reducing monetary growth, at a time when so many decisions had been taken – Clegg, VAT, Nationalized Industry Pricing – which had the effect of increasing the price level, and the demand for money to finance a given level of transactions. Given that the demand for money was rising, restrictive targets for the supply of money virtually guaranteed strong upward pressure on interest rates, which would hardly be conducive to that 'stable environment' which the MTFS was meant to be providing for industry.

Another important point about the MTFS was that it made assumptions about certain key economic relationships which were matters of considerable dispute within the economics profession, and rejected outright by the Keynesians. These included three key propositions: that there was a predictable and causal relationship between changes in the growth of M3 and the rate of inflation; that public sector borrowing was the prime determinant of M3 (as we have already seen, Professor Kaldor, in evidence to the Treasury Select Committee that summer, produced impressive evidence that most of the growth in money supply was the result of bank

advances); and the further view that public sector bor͏
levels were the prime determinant of interest rate ͏.͏ ͏.͏.͏
Experience was very shortly to suggest – or confirm – that all
three propositions were of doubtful validity.

Officials at the Bank of England, whose task it was to carry
out the aims of the strategy in the market place, saw the
MTFS as the first genuine sign that 'this government was
different'. As one commented later: 'It was after that Budget
that I began to take them seriously. They meant it. They were
concentrating on intermediate targets and variables like M3
and the PSBR, and not, like every other government since
the war, on output and employment.' The evangelicals had
at least succeeded in changing the process of policy-making.

Like the National Plan for a time under Labour in the
1960s, the MTFS became a focal point of government policy.
In accordance with how near, or how far, the course of M3 or
the PSBR was from the chosen path, the success, or otherwise, of the government's commitment to monetarism was to
be judged by friend and foe alike. One of the consequent
problems was that believers in, and critics of, the government's monetary policy were often misled as to what was
really going on. Thus the absurd position was soon reached
where the government was simultaneously being told by
hard-line monetarists that it was being too lax, and by critics
that its policy was too tight.

The earliest official concern about the tightness of the
monetary squeeze was to be expressed by the institution
responsible for operating it – namely the Bank of England –
in the summer of 1980.

The March 1980 Budget forecasts had been bleak, pointing
to the sharpest drop in output since the war, and a large rise
in unemployment. But the Chancellor had chosen to maintain
a contractionary fiscal stance, in order to keep the PSBR
down to the chosen target figure in the MTFS. This in itself
meant that the home market for British industry would
remain weak. But two other developments were making life
difficult for industry: the pay explosion in the public sector
was accompanied by a similar burst in the private sector –
thereby weakening industry's competitive position vis-à-vis

other countries; and the exchange rate for the pound was rising, making industry's competitive position even worse. (The fashionable explanations at the time for the strength of sterling were the UK's possession of North Sea oil, and the 'Thatcher factor' – admiration for the Prime Minister's stern policies being reflected in a desire to hold funds in London.)

These developments began to have quite a dramatic impact on the profitability and indeed financial viability of many British companies. To make matters worse, interest rates – as an effect of the monetary squeeze – were very high, energy costs were rising because of the second 'oil shock' of 1979–80, and industrial rates were being pushed up by local authorities as they responded to the central government's financial squeeze by resorting to the best weapon in their power.

The brunt of industry's financial problems was coming from the rise in wage costs (on average some two-thirds of total costs) and the exchange rate. By the end of 1980 British industry was competing against the other leading trading nations on 50 per cent worse terms than in 1977 (as measured by relative unit labour costs, adjusted for exchange rate changes). But at first attention tended to focus on the more obvious irritants: the rate bills, energy costs, and interest rates, independently of the connection the latter might have with the strength of the pound.

By the beginning of July 1980 senior officials in the Bank of England had come to the conclusion that the situation for British industry was becoming intolerable. Short-term interest rates were a crippling 17 per cent; yet if anything went wrong with the M3 figures, interest rates would in theory have to be raised further. This would add directly to industry's interest rate burden, and aggravate the competitiveness problem via the exchange rate.

In addition to being closer to the financial markets, the Bank of England also has a wide range of industrial contacts. The news from these contacts, and analysis of the monetary statistics, showed a consistent picture: British industry was in such dire financial straits that the monetary figures were being heavily inflated by what was known as 'distress borrowing'. Companies were borrowing heavily in order to keep afloat. There was a paradoxical vicious circle: private individuals were putting funds into bank deposits to take advantage of high interest rates, thereby swelling the M3 figure; and companies, faced with high wage bills, were borrowing from the banks, also swelling the M3 figures. But, if interest rates had to be hoisted yet again because of 'poor' money supply figures, would the growth of M3 necessarily slow? The Bank was not at all sure.

Bank officials concluded in July 1980 that the situation was absurd, and that something had to be done to get the government off its M3 hook – to 'de-rate M3' as the objective became known within the Bank. Meanwhile the Bank was effectively undermining the M3 figures it no longer believed in, because through its Industrial Finance Unit and its contacts with the clearing banks it was doing its best to see that good companies were given all the financial help they required to keep them on the road, even if this meant increasing bank advances and hence M3.

This was a characteristically pragmatic response to what the Bank saw as a serious situation; indeed, it feared a rapidly approaching crisis. It would have been politically too embarrassing for the Bank to say publicly what it really thought of the way the MTFS was working within three months of its inception. But the implications of the analysis it was presenting in its quarterly bulletin were first that M3 – the chosen criterion for monetary policy – was dangerously misleading, and second that the exchange rate was too high for British industry to be able to compete successfully. As one senior Bank official subsequently commented: 'In the summer of 1980 you only had to look out of the window to see that monetary policy was too tight.' The height of the exchange rate; the rapid rise in unemployment – up by over 300,000 within twelve months; and other monetary indicators such as M3, all indicated that monetary policy was very strict.

This was the nub of what went wrong under the Thatcher experiment. The inflationary effects of the first Budget were wished away by the belief that they were not really inflationary and monetarism would cope; and monetary policy (as represented entirely, and narrowly, by one definition of money supply), given an impossible job in the circumstances, produced a dangerously tight squeeze on British industry. Industry reacted by cutting back dramatically on its stocks; by closing plant; by borrowing; and by wholesale declarations of redundancies. The monetary policy operated through high interest rates, which had an obvious effect on the cost of borrowing, but, more importantly, served to keep the exchange rate very high during 1979 and 1980 and the early part of 1981, and relatively high thereafter. As one ministerial source put it: 'The monetarists' real problem was that they could not make up their minds whether the squeals from British industry were a good thing or not. They wanted to weed the inefficient out. And even when ICI reported a quarterly loss, some of them thought: "Oh ICI – they're just as bureaucratic as the Civil Service." '

The diagnosis that a vicious circle of high interest rates was attracting money to London and keeping the exchange rate high was not easily acceptable by those who had invested political or intellectual capital in M3, such as Lawson and Burns. It was easier to accept another prevailing view – that the pound was strong because of Britain's possession of North Sea oil. It was argued by proponents of this view either that London was an attractive haven for funds because Britain possessed oil during an energy shortage, or that oil gave such a boost to the balance of payments that the contraction of industry – or 'de-industrialization' – was a necessary counterpart of this.

Both these views tended conveniently to ignore the fact that the government, in accordance with its free market philosophy, was making little attempt to intervene in the exchange markets to stop the pound rising. Nor did they pay much attention to the obvious point that high interest rates were attracting funds to London. There were many other oil-producing countries in the world whose currencies did not seem to be similarly attacked by the energy crisis. And if the economy had been running at a higher level of activity, then the so-called 'inevitable' balance of payments surplus allegedly caused by North Sea oil could have been a lot smaller, offering less justification for the view that Britain somehow needed to de-industrialize in order to avoid having a whopping payments surplus. This latter view, known as the Kay–Forsyth thesis,[5] leapt from the reasonable point that North Sea oil altered the balance between manufacturing and oil in the economy to the illogical conclusion that the absolute size of the manufacturing sector therefore had to shrink. This prompted evangelical ministers to argue for a time that the contraction of Britain's manufacturing base being brought about by their policies was somehow God-given and necessary.

One measure which might have been expected to restrain the rise in the pound was the abolition of exchange controls. This had taken place in the autumn of 1979 within a few months of the Tories' arrival in office. The main political motive for this relaxation was not the height of the exchange rate, however: it was the basic economic philosophy, and the desire to give as free a rein as possible to market forces. If there was one minister who was particularly influential in pressing for this decision, it was John Nott, then at the Department of Trade, who had always held very strong views on the subject. The Bank of England had long been urging the abolition of exchange controls, and restrictions on British companies' financing of operations overseas were gradually being relaxed. The Bank produced technical justifications for a step the government wanted to take anyway.

Those Treasury and Bank officials who were most concerned about the height of the exchange rate in 1979 had hoped that the abolition of exchange controls would calm things down. In fact the pound went on rising during 1980. Outflows of capital took time to gain momentum; meanwhile the high rates of interest available in London were producing offsetting inward flows of short-term capital.

One effect the abolition of exchange control certainly produced was a major upset to the MTFS and the operation of monetary controls. Before the MTFS was unveiled, there had been a system of monetary control known colloquially as 'the corset'. Under this, banks were penalized for allowing their deposits, and hence their lending, to grow above a certain rate. But they had found ways round the controls, by the simple expedient of encouraging the growth of certain categories of asset, notably 'acceptance credits', which had not been included in the original definitions. After exchange controls were abolished, it soon became clear that the corset's days were numbered. As one Bank official put it: 'Why have corset controls in London, if you don't have them in Dublin, and they have all this freedom to do what they like across the exchanges?'

There had been a logical and technical case for dropping the corset in the autumn of 1979, at the same time as exchange controls were abolished. But ministers naturally thought it would look odd to abolish what was theoretically meant to be one of their controls on bank lending and the money supply at the same time as they were hoisting interest rates to 17 per cent. So the decision was delayed even though the British now had the freedom to open bank accounts abroad, well away from the Old Lady of Threadneedle Street's corset controls.

The big question was: what effect would the end of the corset have on the monetary figures? How much bank lending, if any, was not taking place because of the corset? How much was being diverted to other financial assets, such as acceptance credits? And how much would return to the banking system?

Sir Geoffrey Howe was very keen to abolish the corset, and announced in his March 1980 Budget speech that it would go in June. Asked how big or how quick the effect would be on the M3 figures, the Bank of England said they did not really feel able to judge either the size or the timing. There were risks . . . Forced to name a figure, the Bank tentatively said 3 per cent; but, in the words of one official: 'We did not want to be pinned to it.'

This was the harbinger of what turned out to be the worst period of diplomatic relations between a Prime Minister and a Governor of the Bank of England since the days of Harold Wilson and Lord Cromer in the mid 1960s. The pre-Budget debate about the corset was taking place at the same time as the debate over the MTFS and the new monetary targets. If the effect of the corset was underestimated, the monetary targets would look even more vulnerable than they already did under the influence of VAT, Clegg, and so on.

Between the Budget and June 1980 the Bank was able to get a better idea of what the effect of the end of the corset might be. The Governor, Gordon Richardson, had to warn the Prime Minister in June that there might be an explosion of monetary growth as a result of the ending of the corset. But the proof of this was yet to come. The Governor was still able to go to No. 10 Downing Street on 3 July 1980 and say that the corporate sector of the economy was being squeezed to death, and interest rates must come down. The Prime Minister agreed, and the Bank of England's Minimum Lending Rate was reduced by one percentage point to 16 per cent. Whether this was sufficient alleviation for a corporate sector that was being 'squeezed to death' was a moot point. During that first year's wages explosion the sterling /dollar rate had risen from an average of $2.08 in the second quarter of 1979 to $2.28½ in the second quarter of 1980. (And the trend was still strongly upwards.) The 4 July reduction in MLR certainly did not entail a great change of principle because, as it happened, the growth of M3 had been relatively modest in June.

Summer 1980 marked a turning point in relations between the Prime Minister and the Bank. Returning from a meeting with Mrs Thatcher soon after the election, Richardson commented: 'She certainly knows what she wants and she certainly knows how to take decisions.' The evangelicals had come into office thinking of Richardson, as one Bank man put it, as 'a man appointed by Heath who got on well with Callaghan and Healey – what further condemnation did they require?' Yet for the first year or so, although Richardson was not, in Mrs Thatcher's terminology, 'one of us', the No. 10 /Bank relationship proceeded tolerably well, with the Prime Minister often relying heavily on the Governor's advice. Richardson was fluent enough not to be interrupted; would deliver short and effective speeches in her presence; and would stand up to her. He was certainly not cowed by her like some of her close ministerial colleagues.

From the summer of 1980 onwards, wrath towards the Bank of England in general, and the Governor, Gordon Richardson, in particular, was one of the recurring themes of Mrs Thatcher's economic administration. Indeed the relationship between Mrs Thatcher and Richardson proved to be one of the most notoriously difficult areas of diplomacy in her administration. Sir Douglas Wass, the head of the Treasury, also branded as 'not one of us', went through a difficult time with the Prime Minister and was at times by-passed; but he eventually won his way back into her good books. 'She may not like what she thinks are his real views, but she genuinely respects him,' was the way one insider put it later in 1982, when Sir Douglas was shortly due to retire.

But the Governor and Mrs Thatcher could hardly have been better chosen for a personality clash. In the opinion of many who witnessed meetings between them, there was a decidedly mutual lack of respect. The remarkable thing was that they got on so well in the first year. Richardson, a patrician figure, accustomed to the hierarchical nature of the Bank of England, where his word counted, found it difficult to stomach the Thatcher practice of treating ministers and officials alike as if they were schoolboys, and of telling them off in front of their juniors. As one official said, 'I'm not sure which Gordon found more distasteful: having his word questioned by that woman, or being forced by her to eat a cream bun at the end of one of her attacks.'

The balloon went up in early September. The worst figure for M3 after the corset was removed was the 5 per cent growth recorded in July; but it was the holiday season, even for the Prime Minister. The August M3, unveiled in September, showed a further 3 per cent growth. As one official commented dryly: 'It was somewhat unfortunate that the target for the year was only 9 per cent, and that we have had 8 per cent in those two months alone.'

It was also somewhat unfortunate that the next discussions between the Prime Minister and the Bank were conducted in circumstances of high farce. Mrs Thatcher opened an encounter at No. 10 by demanding to know what on earth had been happening to the monetary figures while she had been away,

while Bank officials were anxious to argue the case for a
further cut in interest rates. Since the Bank was losing its
faith in the pre-eminence of the M3 figures, it was not in a
good position to reassure a Prime Minister who had staked
considerable political capital on them. Nor were matters
helped by the fact that at this moment in early September
when Mrs Thatcher wanted to have an inquest on the figures,
neither Richardson nor his deputy, Christopher ('Kit')
McMahon, was immediately available. (Richardson was at a
Central Bankers' meeting in Basel, McMahon at a seminar in
Perugia.)

'Who are these people?' asked an irate Mrs Thatcher when
she came into a room to find John Fforde, then the Bank's
Executive Director, Home Finance, and Eddie George, Deputy
Chief Cashier. Fforde, unaccustomed to Mrs Thatcher's
belligerent manner, was subdued in the subsequent inquest
on the money figures. George did most of the talking – or
rather, the answering, because it was a characteristic of such
meetings with Mrs Thatcher that she herself held the floor.
The two officials were the recipients of the added wrath
caused by the inability of the Prime Minister's office to
summon up Richardson or McMahon in the available time.
The Bank's explanations of why the monetary figures were
so bad – distress borrowing, the difficulty there had been in
forecasting the large impact of the removal of the corset –
were no comfort for a Prime Minister who had allowed
herself to be persuaded that the money supply and M3
should be the cornerstones of her economic policy. At the
end of this strange meeting Eddie George said: 'Nevertheless,
Prime Minister, we shall still have to reduce interest rates.'

By holidaying in Switzerland Mrs Thatcher had certainly
not been getting away from it all. In the course of her holiday
she met Fritz Leutweiler, head of the Swiss Central Bank,
and the economist Professor Karl Brunner of Rochester
University in the US. When she told them her problems the
answer was music to her ears: they both blamed the Bank of
England, saying its method of controlling the money supply
was all wrong. The answer to controlling inflation was to
control the monetary base.

The monetary base is what its name implies: the base of the system. If one thinks of the whole apparatus of bank deposits or credit as an inverted pyramid, at the bottom of the pyramid there are the balances which the banks keep at the Bank of England. Control these, Mrs Thatcher was told, and you have ultimate control of the entire system, because everything the banks can do depends ultimately on these key reserve ratios at the bottom of the pile. Simple, really . . .

The subsequent meeting with George and Fforde was the first of a series of difficult and bitter meetings which brought relations between Prime Minister and Bank, and Bank and Treasury, to a very low ebb indeed. Bank officials in effect said it was ridiculous to try to control the money supply through the monetary base; this was in any case a diversion from the real problem of the economy, which was the existence of a severe squeeze on industry, whatever the monetary statistics showed. Key officials at the Treasury, which at times regards the Bank as politically naive, took the view that it was no good saying the monetary base proposal was ridiculous – governments were always doing ridiculous things: the thing had to be fully explored. And when Mrs Thatcher summoned domestic monetarists such as Brian Griffiths of the City University and Gordon Pepper of the stockbrokers W. Greenwell, she found that each had his own explanation and solution – all different.

During the exploration exercise those Treasury officials who usually have to work very closely with the Bank found their counterparts singularly (and collectively) uncooperative. The theory being examined was that control of the monetary base would lead to control of the entire monetary figures, which would in turn control inflation. The Bank stonewalled with simple questions such as, 'Tell us what the relationship between base money and M3 is . . . we (the experts) don't really know; what we do know is "Goodhart's Law" ' (named after the Bank's eminent monetary economist Charles Goodhart, who had enunciated an economic version of Heisenberg's principle, to the effect that once the monetary authorities tried to control a statistic which in the past might have borne a particular relationship to inflation, its behaviour changed).

What Goodhart and his colleagues argued on this occasion was that the relationship between some of the narrower monetary figures and inflation actually seemed weaker than that with M3. The Bank also had discussions privately with some of the monetarist economists who had been egging the Prime Minister on, and came to the conclusion that they were not very convincing on the supposed relationships.

While this difficult debate was being conducted, life in the real industrial world was not getting any easier. The dollar /sterling exchange rate averaged nearly 10 cents more in the second half of 1980, at $2.38½.

By this time, Mrs Thatcher was being heavily lobbied by industry for interest rate cuts. Although she managed to upstage the CBI's Director General, Terence Beckett, when he threatened a 'bare knuckle fight' over interest rates that October (he emerged from No. 10 saying 'She's a lovely lady'), she was much impressed by what her personal industrialist friends were saying about interest rates, and wanted to get interest rates down.

The most significant single influence on interest rate policy that autumn, however, was probably the announcement of a third quarter loss by ICI. The company's chairman took the unusual – indeed to my knowledge unprecedented – step of going to No. 10 and warning the Prime Minister of how serious the ICI results were going to be. This had a pronounced impact on Mrs Thatcher.

M3 remained the official target, but a cut in interest rates of 2 per cent to 14 per cent was announced on 24 November. The incompatibility of this cut with the strict letter of the M3 formula was explained away by reference to the 'distortions' caused by the removal of the corset, and the argument that the pace of bank lending was showing signs of slowing down. But it was a policy decision on interest rates – in which the Prime Minister played a major role (although the Bank had been urging this too) – which determined the presentation of the background 'causal' factors – emphatically *not* those factors which led to the decision. This episode can be seen as a pragmatic dilution of the pure milk of the M3 ideology. (A number of the more vociferous monetarists at the time were still arguing, on the evidence of the M3 figures, that the squeeze was not tight enough.)

Much work continued after this on the monetary base issue, but nobody could give the Prime Minister what she wanted. In the end, what told against the monetary base system was that nobody could promise her that it would lead to lower interest rates. 'What she really wants,' grumbled one official at the time, 'is a rigid system of monetary control which also brings interest rates down immediately.'

The Bank was in the difficult position of wanting to 'de-rate' M3 while not believing in substituting narrower measures like the monetary base either. This was leading it gradually to a more pragmatic, eclectic view, looking at 'all the aggregates', which would in turn lead to a bigger focus on the exchange rate.

The time was hardly politically ripe for a formal policy change – the MTFS, with its emphasis on M3, was less than ten months old – and the debate was far from over. Conditions were therefore ripe for a classic exercise in compromise and fudging. The search for the Holy Grail continued, with preparations for a Green Paper (a discussion document) on monetary control to be published in the spring of 1981.

Endless technical discussions boiled down in the end to the Bank of England saying to the Prime Minister: 'No country in the world relinquishes control over interest rates, yet that is what you would be asking us to do with a monetary base system.' Concessions were finally made to the evangelical desire for a more market-orientated system with the formal suspension of MLR in August 1981. But there is little doubt that the political desire to influence interest rates won over the monetary base and over proposals to let interest rates be determined entirely by market forces. As one Bank man commented: 'We still show our hand in the market when we want to.'

One monetarist who believed the squeeze was too tight in the autumn of 1980 was the economist Professor Alan Walters. Walters had attracted the attention of Sir Keith

Joseph and Mrs Thatcher some years earlier, as being one of the group of monetarists who had forecast the inflationary consequences of the Heath–Barber boom in the early 1970s. He was consulted by Joseph in 1974, during the period when Sir Keith was reformulating his ideas. Thatcher and Joseph had wanted Walters to be Chief Economic Adviser to the Treasury, well before Burns was approached. But Walters was on a teaching contract in the US at the time. Eventually, however, he was persuaded to come to No. 10 as Mrs Thatcher's personal economic adviser.

Walters was known to belong to the Thatcherite right. A friend of Alfred Sherman at the Centre for Policy Studies, Walters was to become one of the people close to the Prime Minister who liked to describe themselves as 'a line to her conscience' (translated by one of the Tory wets as 'a line to her prejudices'). He took up his appointment at the beginning of January 1981. But news of its imminence leaked out at the end of September 1980. At that time Walters had not been in close touch with British economic policy for several years. But he certainly thought the exchange rate was absurdly high, inclining to the view that 'on purchasing power parity grounds' (comparing the general level of prices and what money can buy in various countries) the pound ought to be nearer $1.70 than $2.40.

Walters's appointment provoked varying reactions. No matter how long it had been planned, and how accidental the timing was said to be, it looked to the outside world as though the Prime Minister, dissatisfied with everyone around her, was 'bringing in her own man'. Reaction in Whitehall varied from 'It's a great insult to Terry Burns' to 'Don't take it seriously, he'll soon be swallowed up by the system.'

Unlike some of those more closely identified with the M3 and MTFS approach, Walters was at least open to the suspicion that monetary policy was too tight. In the October before he took up his appointment he had dinner with John Hoskyns of the No. 10 policy unit, and Alfred Sherman, Director of the Centre for Policy Studies.

Hoskyns was fed up. As we have already seen, he had agreed to join Mrs Thatcher's administration in the belief that the British economy required a tough strategic approach. He tended to talk in meetings of the need to stabilize the situation first, and then – when inflation, public expenditure, the unions, the nationalized industries were under better control – to move on to the economic recovery stage. (There was, others thought, a military air to the way he talked about 'the operation'.) Hoskyns had been appalled by the acceptance of the Clegg commitment. He had urged a wage freeze of some sort right from the beginning, but had received little support. Even the sort of Treasury civil servant who might naturally be in favour of incomes policy had told him, 'It's not on politically.'

After the disaster of Clegg, Hoskyns had had some success in arguing for a tougher pay policy, at least in the public sector. When the pay dam burst in the public sector in the winter of 1979–80, initial Treasury assumptions for the 1980–81 pay round (pay rounds, unlike the financial year, are counted from summer to summer) were of the order of 13 per cent for the public sector. Hoskyns was a member of the camp already referred to who argued that this would make nonsense of the targets in the MTFS right from the start; if the government was serious about wanting to get back on track, it should go for 6 per cent. It was an argument that the Chancellor, Geoffrey Howe, eventually accepted, and the first sign of a change in the monetarists' more naive assumptions about their ability to conquer inflation without some sort of wages policy, if only for the public sector.

Hoskyns had thought that the move towards a strict pay policy for the public sector was a sign that, by the autumn of 1980, things would no longer be out of control. But the lower trend of the pay figure would take time to work through. Meanwhile the inflation figures in the summer of 1980 were at an all-time peak, reflecting the 1979–80 pay explosion.

By the time Hoskyns, Sherman and Walters met that October the scene was dominated by the high interest rates, the strength of the exchange rate, and the agony in the private sector, while the debate between the Treasury and the Bank of England over monetary control was in a state of what one official called 'enraged confusion'. It is perhaps not surprising that Hoskyns is said to have told Walters that evening: 'These people don't know what they are doing. It's a shambles.' Walters was shocked. 'You may find that monetary policy is too tight,' he said. For Walters the combination of the high exchange rate, the rapid rate at which unemployment was rising, and the level of bankruptcies all suggested that the government might have given the British economic system a 'culture shock'. The government might, as it were, have put a bomb under British industry.

As Walters pointed out at the time, the indications were that there had been too severe a monetary contraction – a view very much in accord with what the Bank of England had been saying. He also pointed out that in the end this was a political judgement: there were certainly those on the right who thought 'a bomb under it' was just what British industry needed, John Biffen among them. It was Alfred Sherman who said: 'They all say it's because of North Sea oil that the exchange rate is so high. Let's have an outside study from someone who really knows what he is talking about.' Walters recommended Professor Niehans of Bern University, who was duly commissioned. By the time Walters arrived at his desk in early January 1981 the study had been completed.

The Niehans study was a form of political dynamite. The British government was told to forget the pretext that the high exchange rate was in some way a natural consequence of the oil riches in the North Sea. Money, said Niehans, went where interest rates were, and in the UK interest rates were far too high. Why were they too high? Because monetary policy was too tight. Why was monetary policy too tight? Because in M3 the government had chosen the wrong economic variable to control. Ideally, argued Niehans, they should be trying to control the narrow definition of money – that creature we came across earlier, the monetary base. They should do this, and leave the rest to the market, the Niehans study continued. He could not guarantee that this method would not produce oscillations in interest rates – it certainly would. But if inflation came down, these oscillations would be around a much lower trend of interest rates.

The Niehans study was controversial for many reasons.

From Walters's point of view, it was quite a coup to have commissioned this at Sherman's suggestion and be given confirmation of the scepticism he had expressed way back in the autumn. From the government's point of view, it was helpful in one way to hear from an outside source that the high exchange rate was not a God-given decree. (Of course, many officials knew this. But people in key positions, through a mixture of their ideological beliefs and some misleading economic analysis, did not.)

The Prime Minister herself had been worried about the high exchange rate for some time. The thought that it might be a consequence of her policies did not necessarily prevent her from wanting interest rates and the exchange rate lower without changing the policies. And she certainly found agreeable the argument produced by Niehans that the exchange rate *and* interest rates could be lower without abandoning the basic policy (she was always sensitive to the height of the related mortgage rate).

The obvious problem was that the government had invested so much political capital in M3. Non-monetarists would argue that it was a mistake to invest any monetary statistic with too much political capital. The episode also illustrated the degree to which the Tories were badly prepared in the one economic policy area where they were supposed to be so radically different – namely monetarism.

A seminar was organized among the faithful to discuss Niehans's findings. Samuel Brittan, the economic editor of the *Financial Times* – and, as we have seen, a commentator who had played a major role in influencing the Tories – expressed reservations about Niehans's report (Brittan was one of the many monetarists who had wondered whether the squeeze was tight enough). Niehans said, in one of the great remarks of the Thatcher years: 'Tell me, who are your monetarists in this country? You don't seem to have any.'

But the Walters/Hoskyns camp accepted the Niehans argument. Treasury ministers and the Prime Minister were somewhat hamstrung by the degree of their commitment to M3 and the North Sea argument. As one insider commented: 'It was a hell of a message to swallow. It meant admitting that an awful lot of good companies had gone to the wall for nothing.' At one of the many meetings on the subject in early 1981 it was David Wolfson, Mrs Thatcher's political secretary, who commented: 'If Niehans is right, and monetary policy is too tight, you cannot go on – you must relax.'

During January 1981, when these discussions were taking place, the exchange rate was rising all the time, in terms both of the widely quoted dollar rate and of the so-called effective rate – the average rate against all the leading currencies. This was a period, as we have seen, when some of Britain's leading companies – including ICI – were showing losses, and a number of industrialists, including some of Mrs Thatcher's most ardent supporters, were saying: 'They are overdoing it. We simply cannot live with an exchange rate of $2.40.'

Treasury Chief Secretary John Biffen had played a major role in the VAT decision of the 1979 budget, and Nigel Lawson, Financial Secretary, was the predominant force behind the adoption of the MTFS in 1980. But it was Walters and Hoskyns at No. 10 who were to play the leading role in the spring 1981 Budget – and all as a result of the Niehans study. But the results were not necessarily to be quite as they intended.

The way the Niehans message was interpreted was: 'If he is right, then we have to pave the way for interest rates to fall.' But the crucial point about the way the government went about trying to reduce interest rates was that they still did so within a monetarist framework, or their own version of a monetarist framework. A traditional Keynesian would have argued that the stance of economic policy would have to be relaxed if interest rates were to be brought down. A Keynesian might well concede that there could be an imbalance between fiscal policy and monetary policy – one might be too tight and the other too loose.

On all the familiar measurements, however, fiscal policy had actually been tightened in 1980. This did not prevent people from arguing that the reverse had happened; indeed, just as it was frequently argued that monetary policy was not tight enough before the Niehans study, so it was – often as part of the same argument – maintained that fiscal policy was too loose. Such claims were made, among other places, in the influential *Financial Times* leader columns.

The suggestion that monetary policy might be too tight but fiscal policy too loose became fashionable during the Thatcher years. It had many attractions: it fitted in with the widely prevailing belief that, for all their talk, the Tories had not managed to get public expenditure under control. And it was a convenient excuse for the monetarists when they themselves were criticized. 'If only the government were to spend and borrow less,' they tended to say, 'monetary growth would be on target.' In fact there was much confusion on the subject. For those who wanted savage cutbacks in public expenditure, the latter was always going to appear to be out of control. And every time the so-called wets in the Cabinet defended themselves against Treasury cuts, any victory on their part could be similarly interpreted. Yet the targets for public expenditure and public sector borrowing set by the government were so tight that, even though they were exceeded, the net effect of tax and public expenditure decisions combined was to tighten fiscal policy severely in both 1980 and 1981 (OECD and IMF statistics).

The deflationary stance of policy in the spring 1981 Budget was, by any criterion, a major event for both British and world economic policy. With output falling and unemployment rising fast, here was a government taking measures to make matters even worse. One of the more savagely ironical aspects of this was that the measures which tightened fiscal policy were conceived as being designed to ease the upward pressures on the pound by lowering interest rates, in accordance with the Niehans study.

In other words, the 1981 Budget was in theory designed to alleviate the squeeze on British industry. But while, as we shall see, the pound did come down somewhat from its great heights, the other effect of the Budget was to aggravate the squeeze on domestic demand. And, just to add to the irony of the situation, the fall in interest rates was not destined to last very long.

In 'paving the way for interest rates to fall', the men who

prepared the 1981 Budget were prisoners both of the prevailing monetarist ideology and of the specific straitjacket of monetary targets which we have referred to before. As had become the custom, the basic Budget arithmetic was calculated on the basis of how low the public sector borrowing requirement would have to be if the growth of M3 (notwithstanding Niehans, they stuck to M3) was not to exceed a certain preordained figure (the actual range was 6 to 10 per cent for 1981–82). It mattered not that, in spite of the tightness of policy, the M3 target for the previous twelve months had easily been exceeded. The ritual incantations continued, and obeisance was duly paid to the monetarist god.

According to this arithmetic, things were way out of hand. And, in the view of the monetarists, they were way out of hand because of the public spending trend in general, and the well publicized victory the previous autumn of the wets in the Cabinet debate over public expenditure.

At this point it is worth referring to another plan in the wings, before Walters, Hoskyns and David Wolfson struck with their crucial Budget proposals. This plan came from the Treasury, and was known as the Burns /Middleton hypothesis, after the Chief Economic Adviser, and Peter Middleton, a prominent Treasury official who was heavily involved in all the key aspects of economic policy at this time, and so impressed the Prime Minister that he was early marked out as the likely successor to the head of the Treasury, Sir Douglas Wass, when the latter should retire in 1983. The Burns /Middleton hypothesis should be seen in the context of the Treasury's behaviour in 1979 /80. The Treasury had dutifully advised ministers of the likely consequences for inflation of the June 1979 Budget (the Treasury knew the real world too well to believe that the VAT rise would be offset by price reductions elsewhere, under a pristinely clean monetary policy; it also knew what Clegg etc. had in store for inflation). But that battle fought – and lost – the Treasury became obsessively concerned with the fight against the inflation it knew had been unleashed. This meant that as an institution it largely acquiesced in the rise in the exchange rate, because this was about the one influence which was acting in a contrary direction to the general inflationary trend.

In this acquiescence the Treasury was only endorsing the very strong view of ministers – one insider recalls that, as far as some of the monetarists were concerned in 1979–80, the attitude towards the exchange rate was 'the higher the better'. And in Terry Burns, who arrived at the beginning of 1980, they were reinforced by a man from the London Business School, which had gone out on a limb in favour of strong exchange rate policies (indeed, this was at least one of the reasons why Burns was appointed). In so far as they thought that British industry was suffering in international trade, the Treasury at the time was inclined to blame conditions in the world markets, which were, after all, now suffering from the contractionary policies associated with the second oil shock of 1979–80. (The recession in the rest of the world was much less severe, however.) The connection between the strength of the pound and the impact on British industry had, however, been correctly diagnosed much earlier by the Bank of England, and was something the Governor, Gordon Richardson, emphasized a number of times in private, and more obliquely in public.

The Treasury ministerial team, and monetarists generally, found it difficult to acknowledge the connection between the high exchange rate and the stance of policy. They found it easier to blame the North Sea. But while the machine moved sluggishly towards this acknowledgement, it moved rather faster in seeing the connection between the depth of the British recession, the devastating impact on the profitability of companies and the unemployment trend.

For much of 1980 officials, as well as ministers, had managed to give an impression of complacency in their occasional sessions with the Select Committee on the Treasury. It is, after all, one of their functions to stonewall on behalf of their ministers. But privately they were sharing the concern being expressed about the impact of the squeeze on the corporate sector. If demand was poor and profitability low, where was the much vaunted economic recovery going to come from? On the other hand, they were civil servants, conducting the Thatcher experiment, and at least some of their ministers believed that British industry did need 'a bomb under it' – an approach which one or two of their advisers found morbidly fascinating.

The Burns/Middleton hypothesis was conceived against this background, and with the intention of finding some compromise to alleviate the burden on British industry. It was devised by men who at the time thought the height of the exchange rate was more to do with the North Sea than with the level of interest rates. They were also men closely associated with the monetarist policy, although their friends thought each had some reservations – Burns about the tightness of the PSBR targets, and Middleton more broadly about the degree of the government's dependence on monetarism. Middleton himself was such a quintessentially adept civil servant that, while thought by his friends to have reservations, he was considered by the Prime Minister and the Cabinet to be fully behind all aspects of monetarism.

The Burns/Middleton hypothesis was that, if British industry was suffering too severely as a result of the strength of the exchange rate, and if this was attributable to the North Sea, then the government's tax and royalty revenues from the North Sea should be channelled directly towards relieving this pressure. In particular, they wanted to abolish the employers' national insurance surcharge – a revenue device originally imposed by Denis Healey under Labour which was a tax on employment at a time when unemployment was showing signs of rising much more sharply than anyone had expected; it was not rebateable on exports; it was a tax about which the Confederation of British Industry complained bitterly. Its abolition must be a means by which industry could be given immediate relief. As one insider commented: 'The debate went on far too long inside the Treasury. It was an argument which was won in principle and lost in practice.' NIS was reduced piecemeal over the next few years, and always, it seemed, grudgingly.

Whether the implementation of the Burns/Middleton

proposal would have represented a major change in policy is a matter of debate. It would almost certainly have led to a less sharp rise in unemployment. But it was always up against the government's ambivalent attitude towards industry – at one stage, for instance, the argument against it was that, if employers were in any way let off the hook, they might be encouraged to grant excessive wage claims just when inflation was beginning its long climb down. *A fortiori*, such relief might lead to the conclusion that Mrs Thatcher had lost her determination – that the much sought for U-turn was being made. Mrs Thatcher herself, at least partly under the influence of a few close businessman friends of hers and her husband's, was keener on interest rate cuts: not only would they be politically popular, but they were also being urged by industry, and they could even be presented as a sign that the policy was working.

But the policy was showing every sign of not working. After a meeting at Chequers in mid January 1981, when the prospect for public expenditure was presented, from the government's point of view, as horrendous, the forecasts seemed to get worse week by week. Everybody wanted interest rate cuts, but the extremists had convinced themselves that these could only be achieved through a progressive reduction in the PSBR.

Burns and Middleton would have settled for higher PSBR than the £10½ billion eventually unveiled in the March 1981 Budget. Despite the 'deterioration' in the public spending picture, Sir Douglas Wass, the Treasury's Permanent Secretary at the time, argued that public spending was at last under control. Walters, Hoskyns and Wolfson – much impressed by the Niehans view of the need to achieve lower interest rates, and by the conventional view that this required a cut in the PSBR – came to the view that 'When things are very bad, you have to forecast the forecast.' They feared that whatever Wass argued now, the public spending picture might look worse again in the autumn. They felt the government's credibility over spending cuts was already in question. If there was a 'soft' Budget, and a funding crisis in the autumn, with the government, unable to sell gilts, having to raise interest rates again, then both Thatcher and Howe's positions would be at risk.

In a pre-Budget paper to the Prime Minister and the Chancellor, Hoskyns, Walters and Wolfson urged ministers to go for 'an unthinkably low PSBR'. There were debates in progress as to whether the figure should be £11 billion or £12 billion, and the CBI's pre-Budget representations indicated that, because of the effect of inflation, a PSBR below £15 billion for 1981–82 would imply a fiscal tightening. Hoskyns, Walters and Wolfson urged the lowest possible. It was probably Hoskyns's moment of greatest influence. The man who believed in 'systems analysis' and 'games theory' and wanted to change the politicians' thinking was 'thinking strategically', saying things like 'minimize your maximum regret', and weighing outcomes against strategies a year ahead.

The pre-Budget paper led to what several participants described as 'a rough discussion', at which Prime Minister, Chancellor, Wass and Burns were also present. Hoskyns, Walters and Wolfson said they were not in the business of politics but of risk analysis. One serious risk was the political demise of the Prime Minister and Chancellor if there was a crisis in the autumn. They got plenty of support from the Prime Minister, from Nigel Lawson, and from Geoffrey Howe's political adviser, Adam Ridley, who was himself much impressed by the view that the way to get interest rates down was to have as low a PSBR as possible. The official Treasury side put up a strong defence – the professional civil servants were hardly pleased at what one described as 'a bunch of outsiders calling the shots'. Moreover, the Treasury's own credibility and judgement were at stake, in that the political advisers were urging a strategy essentially based on the view that the forecasts were wrong and the Treasury could not be trusted on public expenditure.

Howe was not known for his speed of decision-making and would often leave a Treasury debate unconcluded, electing 'to sleep on it' when the machine required urgent decisions. But he was, from the start, biased in favour of as low a PSBR as possible, and never gave the impression of even understanding what the debate concerning 'a cyclically adjusted PSBR' was all about. (This, as we have seen, is the concept that a higher PSBR is perfectly acceptable during a recession, because of the tendency of government disbursements on unemployment benefit to rise, and tax receipts to fall.) He also was thought by those closest to him to have a strong stubborn streak – to be inclined to dig himself further into whatever trench he was in. The meeting was described by one of the losers as 'a real cliffhanger'. At the end, Howe said simply: 'I am going to listen to the Jeremiahs, not the voices of comfort.'

So, just as a near doubling of VAT had seemed unthinkable to the Treasury and outside world in 1979, and a deflationary Budget in the face of deepening recession in 1980, so the government reacted with an even tighter fiscal stance when all the outside debate was about how far they should loosen the reins of policy. The tightening of policy was illustrated by the fact that the March 1981 Budget aimed to bring the PSBR down from £13½ billion in 1980–81 to £10½ billion in 1981–82. This meant that, during a recession, the PSBR as a proportion of gross domestic product was to fall from 6 per cent to 4¼ per cent.

As with so many economic policy decisions, there were aspects which pleased nobody, not even the proponents. Both the Treasury and the Bank of England were shocked by the tightness of the 1981–82 PSBR targets at a time when the recession was looking considerably worse than had been threatened a year earlier. The Bank, which had been urging greater flexibility for some time, was increasingly concerned about the viability of large chunks of British industry, and saw precious little alleviation as a result of the 1981 Budget. Although a number of officials in both these institutions had initially acquiesced in varying degrees of Thatcherism, their essentially pragmatic approach told them that things were being grossly overdone. Even Hoskyns and Co., who felt so passionately that the country's basic attitudes needed to be changed, were disappointed in one respect – they wanted a formal increase in income tax to drive home to people the seriousness of the situation as they saw it. But, once presented with the decision to go for a tight PSBR, the politicians believed they would not get an overt increase in income tax through the Commons. They opted instead for suspending the so-called Rooker–Wise/Lawson amendment, under which tax allowances are normally increased each year in line with inflation. (This means of achieving the PSBR targets might have embarrassed a lesser man than Lawson, who had fought passionately for the indexation of tax allowances, and was indeed the very same Lawson of 'Rooker–Wise /Lawson'.)

One insider subsequently commented: 'I was amazed how many people were fooled into thinking this was not a tax increase.' But the wets in the Cabinet were not. They were furious. Once again, the way the Budget cards are kept so close to the Chancellor's chest meant there was little the wets could do about this. But the seeds were certainly sown for a revolt in the area they could influence – the next round of the public expenditure plans.

From the Hoskyns /Walters point of view the 1981 Budget had a twofold aim: 'preventing the government from falling apart' by sticking to a tight fiscal policy; and getting interest rates and the exchange rate down, à la Niehans study. They believed that, in order to get interest rates down, fiscal policy had to be tightened, because the balance of monetary and fiscal policy was wrong, with too much weight being placed on the former. But the basic thinking behind their strategy, and that adopted in the Budget, could not be admitted: the monetarists could not own publicly that they had got their monetary policy wrong.

The episode had many other ironic aspects. The Budget may have been designed in part to alleviate the squeeze on British industry by getting the exchange rate down, but the instrument chosen caused the domestic squeeze to be tightened. The exchange rate did fall sharply between January and September 1981, but towards the end of September there was a panic that things had gone too far: in the US, where monetarism was now also very much in vogue, interest rates had risen so far that money was being attracted away from London in vast quantities. Although the Budget had been designed to avoid a panic rise in interest rates in the autumn, this was exactly what occurred – but for an unexpected reason: a rise in US interest rates. The squeeze on British industry was alleviated somewhat, but there was no significant economic recovery.

Thus the attachment to a lower exchange rate was short-lived. There was fear of a 'free fall' in September 1981 – the effective rate* had come down from 105.6 to 86.6 and the dollar rate from $2.43 to $1.76¾. With high US interest rates and an even stronger dollar, the so-called North Sea factor influencing the pound seemed finally to disappear, and the interest rate argument to strengthen. It was the speed at which the pound was falling in September 1981 which most worried the government and the Bank of England. So, having been concerned about the height of the pound, and allowed considerable adjustment, the policy-makers went back to worrying about the effect of a lower pound on inflation in autumn 1981.

The Bank of England showed its basic interest in the concept of stability. It had been much more unhappy about the previous rise in the pound than the Treasury, and correspondingly it showed much more concern about the autumn 1981 fall. Also, in spite of the depressed state of the economy and its lack of faith in M3 and pure monetarism, the Bank, like the Treasury, became concerned about a swelling in the monetary figures at about the same time. But it was fear about the exchange rate that was the prime reason for the sharp rise in interest rates in autumn 1981. Bank base rates, reduced from 14 per cent to 12 per cent the day after the Budget, were pushed back up to 14 per cent on 16 September and 16 per cent on 1 October.

The success of the 1981 Budget as an instrument to get the exchange rate down via lower interest rates was therefore short-lived. The stance of fiscal policy remained restrictive, and monetary policy was in effect tightened again with the high interest rates in the autumn. Meanwhile, although industry received some relief from the fall in the pound, in the autumn of 1981 sterling was still overvalued by a

* The 'effective' rate is a Bank of England index (1975 = 100) of the pound's value against all the major currencies, not just the dollar.

considerable amount, and the competitive position of British industry remained acute. This is illustrated by the index of 'real' exchange rates published by the American bank Morgan Guaranty Trust. This measures the average exchange rate of each currency, adjusted for inflation differentials. Britain's real exchange rate rose from 106.3 in 1978 (March 1973 = 100) to 118.4 in 1979 and 137.9 in 1980. It had been well over 140 during the heady days of 1981, but was still 135.2 in December 1981. By comparison the indices for France and Germany hardly changed at all during this period – the German real exchange rate was 103.5 in 1978, 103.9 in 1979, 100.8 in 1980 and 98.6 in December 1981. Similarly, the French real exchange rate was 97.4 in 1978, 98.9 in 1979, 100.6 in 1980 and 97.6 in December 1981. Dr Otmar Emminger, former President of the West German Bundesbank, told the Commons Select Committee on the Treasury that the rise in sterling's real exchange rate represented 'by far the most excessive overvaluation which any major currency has experienced in recent monetary history' (October 1982).

Meanwhile the public expenditure negotiations between the Treasury and the Cabinet in the summer and autumn of 1981 once again aroused false hopes of the degree to which the wets were softening the economic squeeze. The collective departmental bids for extra spending in 1982–83 amounted to some £5 billion more than the Treasury wanted. This brought two reactions from the hard-line Thatcher camp. One was a reshuffle – see next chapter – which ensured that the strength of the wets in Cabinet was, as it were, sapped. The second was the familiar response of the Chancellor, namely to ensure that, whatever revisions had to be made to the public spending projections, the net position of fiscal policy – taking spending and revenue plans together – was still restrictive in 1982–83.

The Cabinet meeting of 21 July 1981 was a watershed in the history of Mrs Thatcher's economic administration. Faced with calls for yet another £5 billion of public spending cuts, the Cabinet came as close as it ever did to revolt. Sir Geoffrey Howe made a presentation to ministers in which he outlined his plan for the cuts, while being unable to offer any hope whatever on the output and employment front: indeed, unemployment was, according to the Treasury's July forecasts, going to continue rising indefinitely, although it had already soared by 1 million (to 2.7 million) in the previous twelve months.

The suggestion that, in the face of this bleak picture, there should be further cuts in public spending brought gasps from a number of Cabinet ministers, and cries that enough was enough. Sir Geoffrey's presentation went very badly. Lord Hailsham likened him to President Hoover of the US, who had been considered by many the prime culprit for the inter-war depression. Lord Carrington described it as 'a political disaster'. Sir Ian Gilmour said, 'This points to the decline and fall of the Tory Party.' (It was on another occasion, but to make a similar point about the same policies, that Peter Walker said to Sir Geoffrey: 'This is the economics of the madhouse.') Even John Nott, one of the original monetarists, said Sir Geoffrey had delivered 'a lousy paper'. And John Biffen, former Chief Secretary to the Treasury and now Leader of the House, also opposed the Chancellor. The Prime Minister and the Chancellor only had Sir Keith Joseph and Leon Brittan (who had followed Biffen as Chief Secretary) on their side.

It was as a direct result of this stormy meeting in July that the Prime Minister decided to reshuffle her Cabinet in September 1981. James Prior was exiled from the Department of Employment to be Secretary for Northern Ireland. Sir Ian Gilmour, Lord Privy Seal and Deputy Foreign Secretary, was sacked; so were Mr Mark Carlisle, Education Secretary, and Lord Soames, Leader of the Lords and Lord President of the Council. Norman Tebbit, in the true Thatcher mould, was brought into the Cabinet as Secretary for Employment (he was shortly, at the Tory conference, to become the most quoted man of the Thatcher years with his advice to the unemployed to 'get on your bike' and look for a job). And Nigel Lawson, who had been such an evangelical force at the Treasury – but not previously in the Cabinet – was promoted to Energy Secretary.

Lord Thorneycroft, chairman of the Conservative Party,

was also removed from his post. At 72, Thorneycroft had given indications of wanting to move, but his departure seemed to be accelerated by his disagreement with Sir Geoffrey Howe that the recession was over. (Mrs Thatcher was said by biographers to be an admirer of Thorneycroft, not least for the stand he had taken in resigning from the Macmillan government over public spending cuts in 1958. But Thorneycroft gave the strong impression of being a wet as unemployment mounted under the Thatcher administration; he was also said subsequently to have regretted being persuaded to resign in 1958 by his Treasury Junior Ministers Enoch Powell and Nigel Birch.)

Mr Cecil Parkinson, a Junior Minister at the Department of Trade, was given Thorneycroft's job as chairman of the party, and also given a seat in the Cabinet as Paymaster General. These moves significantly swung the balance within the Cabinet. Before September 1981 only the Prime Minister herself, Howe, Biffen, Joseph, Nott and Howell were true believers. Most of the others had been hostile to, or shown a marked lack of interest in, monetarism. Sir Ian Gilmour's parting shot was: 'It does no harm to throw the occasional man overboard, but it does not do much good if you are steering full speed ahead for the rocks. And that is what the government is now doing.'

With the world recession now getting worse, and little sign of the miraculous incentive effects they had hoped for from British industry, the evangelical ministers approached the 1982 Budget with the feeling that, if they were in for a penny, they might as well be in for a pound. They were unpopular with the industrialists who traditionally supported them; unemployment was at previously unthinkable levels; the government had taken a battering in the opinion polls. The feeling was that they were too far gone to turn back, and that falling inflation was the one solid hope they could eventually deliver to the electorate; the rest – for all the boasts about improvements in productivity and so on – were to be benefits on the horizon. Against this sombre background, the subsequent emphasis on privatization and anti-union legislation was, at least in part, seen by the

Economic Strategy Committee as a useful public diversion from the fact that the 'real economy' was in such a dire state.

Reinforced by the September Cabinet reshuffle, the Chancellor announced measures on 2 December 1981 to increase charges and national insurance contributions in the 1982–83 financial year in order to offset about half of the extra £5 billion public spending which had been the subject of the July Cabinet row.

The Walters/Hoskyns Budget of 1981 had aimed to bring the PSBR down from £13½ billion in 1980–81 to £10½ billion in 1981–82. This, as we have seen, was a remarkably restrictive move at a time when unemployment was rising sharply and there was no sign of any significant recovery in output. The 1982 Budget kept the pressure on: although the monetary targets (once again exceeded in 1981–82) were relaxed, and extended to include other measures than M3, Sir Geoffrey still aimed at a further cut in the PSBR to £9½ billion.

One of the more ironic postscripts on the Chancellor's Budget strategy was written in the early summer of 1982, after the 1982–83 Budget proposals had been unveiled. The Treasury revealed that the figure for 1981–82 had been revised, and that the PSBR had worked out at only £9 billion – £1½ billion less than the £10½ billion target on which the 1981 Budget had been based. This meant that the 1981 Budget was even more restrictive than had been intended – or alternatively, that the panic that spring had been entirely unnecessary. Those who doubted the forecasts had themselves failed 'to forecast the forecasts'.

It is also worth noting that the country had become so accustomed to Sir Geoffrey's medicine that his 1982 Budget went down surprisingly well in Parliament and press, despite the fact that fiscal policy remained tight: such 'concessions' as there were were offset in the overall arithmetic by restrictions elsewhere.

The apparent relaxation of the government's monetary policy in the 1982 Budget led many people to believe that monetarism was now dead. But the PSBR targets demonstrated that the fiscal squeeze was still very severe. The impact of the 1981 Budget squeeze was summarized by the OECD: 'Allowing for the impact of automatic stabilizers' (that is, the tendency for tax revenue to fall and social security spending to rise during a recession), 'the cyclically adjusted budget tightening is estimated at about 3½ per cent of GDP, the largest in the OECD area and significantly more than had been budgeted for.' That was 1981–82; the OECD estimated that the 1982 Budget implied further tightening of fiscal policy, on the same basis, for 1982–83.

After the March 1982 Budget there was a curious ambivalence about economic policy. The prospect of an election can be seen as an influence from then on – not, it must be stressed, on any change in the fiscal stance, but on the presentation of such concessions as there were. This was particularly so in the change of emphasis at the Department of Industry, where the arrival of Mr Kenneth Baker as a junior minister with a particular brief for promoting 'information technology' led to a whole series of announcements giving the impression that the Cabinet was spending money right, left and centre. Up to a point it was – in this particular area: indeed, the Prime Minister herself was to be pictured alongside new computers installed in schools; she seemed to see no irony in boasts about the way the government was spending money on new electronic gadgets for the very same schools that were suffering from cuts in their allocations for textbooks.

This 'positive' approach to industrial intervention was, of course, in marked contrast to the Friedman /Hayek /Joseph philosophy with which the government arrived in 1979. It had ended up spending billions of pounds in support for the steel, coal and motor industries. But its support and intervention were in nearly all cases given reluctantly and after much agonizing. In bailing out such giant concerns as British Steel and BL, the government were also backing men at the helm whom they trusted, men recruited from the private sector, such as Ian MacGregor and Sir Michael Edwardes.

The agony of the evangelicals over this was seldom better

illustrated than when Sir Keith Joseph, while at the Department of Industry, circulated a paper to his Cabinet colleagues on the economy sub-committee arguing that a request for financial help from BL should be granted, and that the company should not be allowed to collapse. The paper pointed to the ramifications for the Midlands components industry, which had obvious political implications for the Conservatives in an area where they had won a number of key marginal seats in 1979. The paper was circulated over a weekend, and one of the wets commented: 'At last Keith is beginning to see sense.' The following Monday, when the committee met to consider Sir Keith's paper, he said: 'Prime Minister, I am afraid that after much reflection I have to disagree with the arguments of my own department, and urge you not to let this go through.' But Mrs Thatcher and her colleagues had digested the political implications and Sir Keith's agonized plea against his own proposal was dismissed.

It might be said that such changes of policy were U-turns; but in budgetary terms they were at the price of spending elsewhere in the economy. Such support tended to be justified – or rationalized – by some members of the Treasury as a reasonable use of North Sea oil revenue, given that it was possession of North Sea oil which allegedly caused the pound to rise, and aggravated the trading problems of these industries. But, as we have seen, even the evangelicals eventually questioned the North Sea explanation.

Sir Geoffrey presented the 1982 Budget against the background of many a ministerial promise that economic recovery was on the horizon. The problem was that it stayed on the horizon. People were certainly looking out for the recovery; gross domestic product had fallen some 5 per cent between 1979 and 1981, and manufacturing output alone had dropped by as much as a fifth. Sir Geoffrey gave a forecast of 1½ per cent growth of GDP for 1982; but it turned out to be a mere ½ per cent. And despite repeated ministerial claims to the contrary, manufacturing output remained virtually flat throughout 1982.

The Falklands War of April–May 1982 was, among other

things, a convenient diversion from the absence of the promised economic revival. Considerations of the effect on the PSBR did not enter into the conduct of the war (although they had led to defence economies, such as the withdrawal of *Endurance*, which misled the Argentines into thinking that Britain would not retaliate).

One of the most significant economic events of 1982, which passed relatively unnoticed, was a concession to the industrial lobby. Although the government had for much of the time seemed grudging in its help to industry – the employers' national insurance surcharge was never abolished, merely reduced in dribs and drabs – suddenly, in July 1982, it completely abolished official hire purchase controls. Taken in conjunction with a great and largely successful effort by the banks to corner a section of the home loan market (by no means all of which finance was spent on the purchase of houses), this contributed to the revival of consumer spending in the second half of 1982 and the first half of 1983.

Another major factor leading to a revival of consumer spending was a recovery in real incomes – that is the real incomes of those who were not unemployed – in the first half of 1983. This reflected the fact that the rate of inflation, now down to 4 to 5 per cent, was several per cent below the increase in average earnings. And, on top of this, consumer spending was fuelled by a fall in the percentage of incomes saved.

But the benefits of this revival of demand to British industry appeared strictly limited in 1982, when real demand rose by 2½ per cent but domestic output by only ½ per cent. (The wisdom of abolishing h.p. controls when British industry was still so uncompetitive had been questioned by Treasury officials in July.)

To the extent that British industry participated in this upturn, in 1982 it did so by drawing on its stocks of goods. There was no sign of any recovery in manufacturing output until 1983, and by the end of the first quarter there had been only the faintest glimmer of an upturn. Moreover, although there was once again much politically inspired talk of industrial recovery, expectations were very muted. When Sir Geoffrey Howe unveiled his March 1983 Budget, he confirmed that the growth of GDP had, after all, only been ½ per cent in 1982; and although he forecast growth of 2 per cent for 1983, the rise in manufacturing output alone was only expected to be about 2 per cent or so (after its 20 per cent fall), and unemployment was forecast to go on rising.

The 1983 Budget was widely expected to be the last before the general election, and so it proved. Many also expected an 'electioneering' Budget. In this they were disappointed – or were they? One crude political justification for another of Sir Geoffrey's cautious budgets was that any reflation at this stage was unlikely to have any impact on the unemployment figures before the election. At all events, once again, even with an election on the horizon, Sir Geoffrey stuck ostensibly to the path of what the Prime Minister and he regarded as fiscal rectitude. He was even able to announce that the policy of holding down the PSBR in 1982–83 had been so successful that many departments had 'underspent'. The 1982–83 PSBR was estimated to have been £7½ billion instead of £9 billion. (In the run-up to the Budget the country was treated to the rare sight of Treasury ministers – evangelicals at that – exhorting public sector departments to spend more – or, rather, to underspend less.)

The squeeze looked so tight that Sir Geoffrey was able to announce a 12 per cent rise in tax allowance (compensation, but with two lost years in between, for the failure to index personal allowance in the 1981 Budget) while still aiming to hold the PSBR at £8 billion in 1983–84. There were various electoral sweeteners, including a proposed rise in the limit on mortgage relief from £25,000 to £30,000 (the latter was at the Prime Minister's insistence). But the concessions depended on some smart work with the figures. It was 'assumed' that 'underspending' would continue – in spite of exhortations to the contrary. And an unusually low figure was produced for the 'contingency reserve'.

The March 1983 Budget was a balancing act in more senses than one. The Prime Minister and Chancellor wanted to please the electorate while appearing to stick to their fiscal

guns, and they had an added motive in the latter aim, in not
wanting to upset the foreign exchange markets; for the
months October 1982 to February 1983 had seen another
devaluation of sterling. After the exchange market panic of
September /October 1981, the government had kept the
pound's average value within a narrow range of 88 to 92 of
its effective index (1975 = 100). Although the existence of
this 'target range' was steadfastly denied, it was quite clear
that the Treasury /No. 10 /Bank of England triumvirate responsible for tactics in the foreign exchange markets were gearing
their operations to such an end.

For a whole year monetary and exchange rate policy was
to edge interest rates down when this was compatible with
exchange rate stability, and provided that the monetary
figures – however discredited they might have become –
were within the re-based target range set at the time of the
Budget. However, as it became increasingly apparent that
the economy in general and industry in particular were not
recovering, officials once again became more and more
concerned about the strength of the pound. It was possible to
deduce from a reply given in November by Terry Burns, the
Chief Economic Adviser, to the Treasury Select Committee,
that the possibility of a 5 to 10 per cent devaluation was at
least under consideration. (Mr Peter Shore, Labour's Shadow
Chancellor, made his contribution to the debate by suggesting that a devaluation of nearly 30 per cent was needed if
Britain's trading competitiveness was to be fully restored.)
The Treasury also highlighted, in its November 1982
'Autumn Statement', both the competitiveness problem and
a forecast of zero balance of payments surplus in 1983, at the
existing exchange rate, notwithstanding the by now huge
contribution to the balance of payments from the North
Sea.

The Treasury's statement made no bones about the competitiveness problem:

Over the past five years or so, and partly reflecting the poor level of
competitiveness, UK industry has lost a share in both overseas and
domestic markets. Between 1977 and the first half of 1982, the

volume of world trade rose by a total of about 18 per cent, while UK exports of manufactures were unchanged. In the domestic economy over the same period, the demand for manufactures changed very little; but import volumes rose 40 per cent, while output of the UK manufacturing sector fell 14 per cent.

The argument for a further devaluation was that it was necessary for industrial recovery. This was probably the predominant view of the official Treasury and a number of Bank of England officials. The argument against a devaluation was that, apart from the much-trumpeted gains in productivity (an object of dispute, and not exactly a good subject for the hustings), the government's most tangible claim to economic success at this stage was the reduction in the rate of inflation. A devaluation could, via higher import prices, send the fall in the rate of inflation into reverse, and thus jeopardize even this achievement.

Having shown so much concern about the adverse effects on industry of the 1979–80 rise in the pound, the Governor of the Bank of England now showed that institution's basic preoccupation with 'stability' by arguing against a deliberate devaluation in the autumn of 1982. This reinforced the political instincts of the Prime Minister, and there the matter rested – for a time.

When news of the internal debate seeped out, the foreign exchange market took the matter into its own hands, and the pound fell. This of course suited the devaluation school fine – provided the fall should not get out of control: memories of the collapse of sterling under Labour in 1976 died hard, and memories of the dangers of a 'free fall' in September /October 1981 were still fresh. Internal Whitehall calculations now showed that, with the economy so depressed, and importers doing so well, the inflationary consequences of a 10 per cent fall in the pound might not be very great.

Bank base rates, after being reduced from 14 per cent to 12 per cent at the time of the March 1981 Budget, had, it will be recalled, been lifted to 14 per cent and then 16 per cent in the autumn sterling crisis. They had edged down to 13½ per cent by the time of the Chancellor's March 1982 Budget, when they were further reduced to 13 per cent. The policy of edging interest rates down provided the exchange rate was not disturbed brought base rates to 9 per cent by November 1982. Controlling the slide in the pound during the period November 1982 to March 1983 involved a base rate rise to 10–10¼ per cent in December and to 11 per cent in January 1983, and the loss of 10 per cent of the official foreign exchange reserves (which fell from $18.5 to $16.6 billion between end October and end February).

It was a principal aim of the 1983 Budget to steady the foreign exchange markets. The government did not want an old-fashioned sterling crisis on its hands in the run-up to the election (but they were prepared to blame any such crisis on Peter Shore's advocacy of a large devaluation, and, if it suited, to cite such a crisis as justification for an early election, 'to resolve uncertainty').

At one stage (24 March 1983) the devaluation since the autumn had been nearly 15 per cent. On Budget day, 15 March, it was assumed for forecasting purposes that the devaluation would remain at around 10 per cent. The pound recovered in the period up to the declaration of the general election on 9 May, to the point where the devaluation since the autumn averaged only about 7½ per cent, and bank base rates were still 10 per cent.

The 'recovery' in the pound did not necessarily bode well for the strength of the hoped-for recovery in the real economy. The CBI was promulgating for all it was worth the result of its spring survey of industrial trends, showing that output was at last picking up, and that business confidence was at its highest for several years.

With inflation in the 4 to 5 per cent range (although forecasts abounded of a rise to 6 to 8 per cent by spring 1984), with a *belief* that recovery was coming, and with the summer school-leavers not yet on the unemployment register, the basic problems of a deflated and still deeply uncompetitive economy were for a time concealed. It was the perfect moment, from an economic policy point of view, to call an election, because things were almost bound to look worse in the autumn, and the chickens had not yet come home to roost.

As Chancellor, Sir Geoffrey Howe was rarely so influential with the Prime Minister as when he joined the chorus which insisted, when she was indecisive, that there should be a June election.

REFERENCES

1. *Who Runs the Economy?* (1979).
2. *Mrs Thatcher's First Year* (1980).
3. *Observer*, 9 January 1983.
4. The Scourge of Monetarism (1982).
5. P. J. Forsyth and J. A. Kay, Institute of Fiscal Studies (1980).

CHAPTER SIX

WHY?

We are left with several important questions. How did the Thatcherites get away with it? And, in refusing to be deflected from their course, were they actually still on the right course, or had they lost sight of their objectives in their stubborn determination not to be seen to be weakening? For instance: during 1983 Mrs Thatcher was receiving great accolades for her determination. She had stuck to her guns; there was no U-turn away from the deflationary direction in which her economic policy had been heading. Yet the revival of entrepreneurial initiative was conspicuous by its absence; there was a growing perception that, for all the promises, the tax burden was higher than when she had taken office; and there was still great Conservative concern about the level of, and direction of, public expenditure.

In seeking the answers, we must be mindful of the background to Mrs Thatcher's rise to power and her determination never to be seen to do a U-turn in the manner of Edward Heath. We should perhaps also recall Professor Galbraith's argument that, if you are going to be so foolish as to conduct a monetarist experiment, what better people to try it on than the British, whose famous phlegm will put up with anything?

At the very simplest level, the Thatcherites got away with it because they seized the reins of power over economic policy, and kept them. They kept them partly because of the way economic power is allocated in Britain, and partly because — although they had a few scares — nothing happened to panic them. Throughout the period 1979–83 there were many observers who expected them to be diverted from their course, but the expected event did not happen. What did happen were a number of deviations and adjustments. These were seized upon by observers at the time as indications of a U-turn, but they were nothing of the sort. Indeed they were a necessary corollary of Mrs Thatcher's determination not to conduct a major U-turn.

The power structure of economic policy in Britain is very much in favour of a determined Prime Minister and Chancellor. The Treasury gives the predominant economic advice, but civil servants are not called civil servants for nothing, and they listen to their master's – or mistress's – voice. Those civil servants who disagree too much, or do not cooperate, easily find themselves exiled. And the key decisions are made either by the Chancellor and the Prime Minister, or by a Cabinet committee which they can nominate to suit themselves.

Every such policy decision is presented to Parliament as a *fait accompli*. Provided the Prime Minister has a reasonable majority in the House, most measures get through without too much difficulty. Such changes as Parliament makes tend to be in the area of detail rather than of overall policy, and it is with the overall policy that we are primarily concerned. All those *ad hoc* decisions about the exchange rate in 1979 and 1980, for instance, were made well away from the floor of the House – and indeed from the Cabinet table. The 1982 Budget, with its many small proposals, was discussed at length in the Commons, but most members did not seem to be able to distinguish the wood (no change in the fiscal policy stance) from the trees (many small measures, costing the Chancellor little).

This is not to say that individual members of the House did not pour devastating criticism on the government from time to time. I recall, in particular, a debate on unemployment when both James Callaghan and Edward Heath made speeches in quick succession which would have moved anybody but an evangelical to reconsider his beliefs. In the Lords, Lord Kaldor, among others, made withering attacks on the government (subsequently published as *The Economic Consequences of Mrs Thatcher*).

Perhaps the most telling criticism of all came from the all-party select committee on the Treasury. Even though its Tory members felt they had to show loyalty to their leader, the themes of excessive deflation and unprecedented loss of competitiveness were picked up and hammered home in questions to distinguished witnesses and in the publication of various reports.

When it comes to the *effectiveness* of this committee, then, alas, the results speak for themselves. This was partly because it was divided at crucial moments – the Tory members wanted to complain about high levels of public expenditure, even if the committee's inquiries suggested that there was a powerful fiscal squeeze. There was also the loyalty point mentioned above. But what the saga really showed up was the constitutional weakness of these committees, relative to their counterparts in the US, when it came to the key questions of power and influence. (When the committee published a report, in the middle of the 1983 May/June election campaign, which was devastatingly critical of the government's fiscal and exchange rate policies, the Tory members immediately tried to disown it.)

As for the wets, in a sense the wets were wet, or powerless, before they started. They were kept well away from the main areas of economic policy, and they had their own departments to run. It takes quite an effort to overturn the policy of another department (even such an economic thinker as Anthony Crosland had found this under the Labour administration during the 1976 sterling crisis). Emasculated by the power structure from the start, the wets were trodden down further as time went on. Their main chances to influence policy always lay on the public spending side rather than with taxation, for the latter is entirely within the Treasury's gift; the former, while under its control, depends to a considerable extent on how hard departmental ministers fight.

One problem with rebelling over public expenditure was the fact that the wets were after all Tories. A bias of some sort against public expenditure has been the mark of many a Tory administration: the question is the degree to which they are against it. Seeing one's departmental budget cut, or not increased enough, is, however, a blow to the virility of even the most determined opponent of public spending – once he actually finds himself running a department. Mrs Thatcher tried to counter this by turning the argument on its head – that the degree to which spending cuts were implemented would itself be a test of virility. One could think of many metaphors to describe the problem with this argument – let us just say it went against the grain. Michael Heseltine, at the Department of the Environment, ploughed his own furrow, being, it seemed to his colleagues, occasionally wet but often dry. Thus he himself had an obsession with cutting back the number of civil servants in his department (virility of a sort, but also tending to cut back his own budget); but the Treasury considered him a profligate spender in other areas, and very lax with the local authorities.

Whatever their natural bias against public spending – and some, such as Peter Walker, did not have such a bias at all – the wets soon began to revolt when they saw the size of the cuts that were, time and time again, demanded of them. As the recession bit deeper, it became clear that the government was running fast in order to stand still: the recession was raising the cost of social security disbursements and reducing tax revenues, but the Chancellor wanted further and further cuts in basic programmes.

As early as spring 1980, Sir Ian Gilmour (Deputy Foreign Secretary, and not in an economic department) was making protests in 'code' with reference to the true nature of Conservatism. Norman St John-Stevas made similar speeches. Both were fired from the Cabinet, and eventually Gilmour's speeches became a lot less coded. He made some particularly fluent and cogently argued attacks on what his colleague, Peter Walker, still in the Cabinet, dubbed the 'economics of the madhouse', calling for reflationary measures, including sensible public expenditure projects of a Keynesian kind to expand demand and create jobs. He subsequently outlined his ideas in an outstanding critique of monetarism called *Britain Can Work* in spring 1983.

One criticism made of the wets by the evangelicals – and

by some officials – is that they were not properly organized, failed to present their case coherently, and so on. There is something, but not everything, in this argument, which comes from sympathizers with the wets as well as their opponents.

It is very easy for civil servants with teams of economists at their disposal to dismiss outside criticism. The Treasury machine is certainly adept at presenting its own case. One of the features of the Thatcher / Howe economic overlordship, for instance, was the sheer weight of speeches and propaganda – the frequency with which phrases such as 'we cannot just print money', 'public sector spending will crowd out private sector spending' and 'there is no alternative' were uttered; there was also the apparent ease with which the evangelicals were able to remove certain categories of people from the unemployment register with hardly a public complaint.

By comparison, speeches by critics such as Gilmour were occasional. And, just to make sure, the Chancellor's office frequently invited potentially doubting back-bench Tory MPs into No. 11 to back up their case. Whether these MPs were blinded with science, or simply flattered by the Chancellor's attention, one does not know (probably both). But in the opinion of the Chancellor's close advisers this helped them to counter the wets' case.

The evangelicals bought a lot of time by always seeming to have an answer to the wets. Occasionally their answer was stronger than words: they hit back with countervailing action. The answers took two distinct forms: the 'pretext', and the 'light at the end of the tunnel' argument. The great pretext of 1979–80 was that wages had nothing to do with inflation; of 1980–81 that the height of the exchange rate was the inevitable consequence of possession of North Sea oil, and there was nothing the government could do about it; of 1981–82 that Britain's problems were the fault of the world recession, and little could be done about that. (This succession of excuses provided a strange accompaniment to the themes of resolution and determination which struck such a chord with the general public.) 'Light at the end of the tunnel' was offered in the form of repeated forecasts of an economic recovery and upturn. These went on for several years, perhaps the most notorious example being the claim by the relatively new Chief Secretary to the Treasury, Leon Brittan, in spring 1982 that 'The signs of recovery are all around us.'

I am not suggesting that the wets were fooled by all of this. But there were certainly times when some of them wanted to believe that, in spite of the nonsenses they thought were being perpetrated, there might be something in it all. And there was a natural inclination on the part of some not to rock the boat. (All were genuinely worried about the economy and the unemployed.) But the most important points about the failure of the wets were their relative powerlessness (already referred to above), and the fact that they did little to counteract this. Their opposition was not organized consistently enough. This argument applied a fortiori as various wets were dropped or resigned from the Cabinet.

Lord Carrington was certainly a wet. He was also, at the Foreign Office, one of the busiest Cabinet ministers. And he made no pretensions to great economic expertise. Lord Soames was a wet, but not in an economic department, and disappointing, from the wets' point of view, when it came to speaking up in the Cabinet. Soames was removed in the reshuffle of September 1981 and Carrington resigned over the Falklands crisis. Mark Carlisle at Education, another quiet wet, also lost his job in that reshuffle. Francis Pym, first Defence Secretary and then Foreign Secretary, was associated with occasional 'coded' speeches, but had little impact at close quarters in presenting the wet case to the Prime Minister. 'Francis is unhappy with the course the economy is taking, but does not seem to know what he wants,' said a colleague in early 1981. Lord Hailsham, the Lord Chancellor, expressed his doubts from time to time, and rallied round the other wets in the various revolts over public expenditure. But this scion of the traditional Tory Party also rallied round Sir Geoffrey Howe with a speech showing fulsome support of the government's economic policies in September 1982, as a row over the future of the welfare state was brewing.

The principal wets were Jim Prior, Peter Walker, Sir Ian Gilmour, Michael Heseltine (from time to time), and Norman St John-Stevas, Chancellor of the Duchy of Lancaster and Minister for the Arts. Stevas, too, made Disraeli-type speeches. He was vociferous at times in Cabinet and was sacked before the others in January 1981, but made a speech supporting the Budget of 1982. Gilmour, who spoke up inside and outside Cabinet, as we have seen, was also sacked in September 1981 but continued his campaign in speeches and newspaper articles afterwards. By summer 1982 a quarter of the original Cabinet had been removed. But not only had many wets gone: the Thatcher/Howe faction in the Cabinet had been strengthened by the arrival in full Cabinet of Nigel Lawson (autumn 1981), Leon Brittan, and Norman Tebbit, at Employment. Moreover in the same reshuffle Prior had been banished to the Northern Ireland department.

There were much publicized revolts by the wets over the scale of public expenditure cuts in the summer and autumn of each of the years 1979, 1980 and 1981. Concessions were certainly won, and public expenditure plans were pruned back somewhat as a result. By the summer of 1981, when departmental bids by the wets and others exceeded Treasury plans by some £5 billion for the following financial year 1982–83, the Prime Minister had finally had enough. The summer revolt, as we saw in Chapter Five, led directly to the autumn Cabinet purge.

The regular revolts of the wets may have been an irritant to a Prime Minister and a Chancellor who already were being criticized by the party faithful for the level of public spending (while the wets thought it too low, given the degree of recession, the faithful always wanted further reductions). In fact, however, the Thatcherites had always got their own back. The revolt of 1979 was followed by the imposition of the Medium Term Financial Strategy in the 1980 Budget. The revolt later that year was considered something of a minor triumph by the wets – they did get some of the public spending cuts restored – but it was followed by the refusal to index tax allowances in line with inflation in the 1981 Budget.

Time and time again, as unemployment crossed the 'politically impossible' thresholds of 2 million, 2½ million, 3 million, Labour failed to provide effective opposition to what was going on. It is not the purpose of this book to inquire into the causes of Labour's problems at this time, or to give an answer to questions such as 'Were its problems terminal?', 'Was the drift to the left inexorable?', or 'Was the main trouble the allegedly ineffectual leadership of Michael Foot?' What is relevant, however, is that Labour was in a pitiful state for most of the period 1979–83, and this, by strengthening the political position of the government and of Mrs Thatcher, also served to underpin her economic policies. It meant, as the Tories recaptured their early losses in the opinion polls, that the wets could make diminishing use of the argument: 'If you do not change course, we shall lose the election.'

The slogan 'there is no alternative' – always logically indefensible – began to be applied not only to economic policies but also to political parties, with each assertion seeming to augment the other: 'there is no alternative policy' became 'there is no alternative government' which in turn became 'there is no alternative economic policy'.

During 1981 the internecine strife within the Labour Party gave rise to the birth of the Social Democratic Party and the SDP/Liberal Alliance. Here was a grouping which attracted a lot of support from middle-of-the-road economists such as the Nobel Prize winner James Meade, and industrialists such as the chairman of ICI, Mr John Harvey-Jones. It offered alternative economic policies: it showed that a party did not have to threaten wholesale nationalization and withdrawal from the EEC in order to provide a different approach to Mrs Thatcher's; it also bit the bullet in stressing that an incomes policy of some sort was a prerequisite of an expansionary programme which would comprise a reflationary package and a depreciation of the exchange rate.

But after initial by-election successes, the Alliance seemed to be preoccupied by internecine struggles of its own. And although its alternative economic policies were little different from those urged by the Tory wets, the latter faced little temptation to make the fateful leap from comfortable office to membership of a fledgling opposition party that might never get off the ground. They would have given up a lot, and risked more, by leaving their beloved party; they opted, not surprisingly, to continue trying to work from within. As one of them commented to me at the time: 'The Conservative Party has been hi-jacked, and we have got to get it back.'

This meant that although excited wets – and journalists – tried to read signs of a U-turn into the various public spending revolts (Independent Television devoted a whole programme to a reconstruction of the revolt of 1980), the basic stance of policy remained the same.

It was only during the public spending rows that the wets gave the impression of working as a team. At other times their criticisms were fragmented and uncoordinated. Even on occasions such as powerful debates on unemployment in the Commons, the impression was that the wets were letting off steam, but did not have a coordinated plan.

The wets who carried the heaviest weight in economic matters were Prior, Walker, Gilmour and Heseltine, when he was being wet. The degree to which they could cooperate must have been limited to some extent by their own separate ambitions – Prior, Walker and Heseltine might all be reasonably thought to have seen themselves as candidates for Prime Minister one day.

The Tories fell sharply in the opinion polls during 1981 and had only recovered slightly before the Falklands War of April–May 1982. The war was so good for the fortunes of their Prime Minister and the party in the opinion polls that the phrase 'Falklands factor' was almost enough, during the rest of 1982, to stop any discussion of the chances of changing economic policy in its tracks.

Buoyed up by the Falklands factor, their success in the opinion polls, and their achievement in avoiding a major U-turn, the evangelicals felt very much in the ascendancy during the summer of 1982. Although the usual painful discussions had gone on between departments and in Cabinet about public spending prospects for the following financial year, there was nothing resembling a revolt on the part of the demoralized wets at the usual June–July spending discussions.

The inclination of Mrs Thatcher, Sir Geoffrey Howe and Sir Keith Joseph was now to go further in the direction of those nineteenth-century liberal beliefs than had so far been possible. The main rival to Sir Geoffrey – John Nott, another nineteenth-century liberal – had fallen by the political wayside and been told he would not get the Chancellorship. From at times seeming to be a liability to Mrs Thatcher because of his dull presentation of the policies, Sir Geoffrey had made a comeback. He was considered to have handled the 1982 Budget speech well – 'his last chance', in the view of one Thatcherite. Howe was officially given the job of co-ordinating policy for the next election manifesto, and in July made a speech in Cambridge which indicated his intention of moving further along the route favoured by the Institute of Economic Affairs – more denationalization of industry; an extension of private medicine; the introduction of educational vouchers – a scheme allegedly widening parental choice in education; and more anti-union legislation.

Sir Geoffrey often gave the impression that almost any prospective measure was a logical progression from a stance he had taken in a Cardiff speech in 1955. To more cynical observers, the government's emphasis on the twin themes of more anti-union legislation and more 'privatization' of publicly owned industries had, since the summer of 1981, seemed a deliberate diversion from the problems of the real economy, of low output and rising unemployment. But the evangelicals set great store by these 'free market' policies.

At the Cabinet meeting on 13 September 1982, Sir Geoffrey presented a gloomy paper arguing that, on existing projections of negligible economic growth during the eighties, yet more dramatic cuts would have to be made in public expenditure if taxes were not to rise sharply. On one projection income tax could rise to a standard rate of 45 per cent, and VAT to 25 per cent. The same Cabinet meeting had also presented the Think Tank's deliberations, which included proposals for the abolition of the National Health Service, and the virtual end of state funding for higher education as well. These papers were too much for the wets, and – led by Peter Walker – they refused to consider the Think Tank paper, saying it was not worth discussing, and a guaranteed election-loser. As for the Treasury paper, Michael Heseltine said: 'Isn't it time the Treasury applied its tiny collective mind to promoting growth, instead of bewailing its absence?'

Apart from anything else, the 1979 manifesto had promised that the grandiose plans for reducing taxation and public expenditure would leave the Health Service intact. The revolt went on for some weeks, and the issue dominated the Tory Party conference at Brighton in early October. But although the Prime Minister spoke then of there being no question of tampering with the National Health Service, Sir Geoffrey was, within days, to be seen on television calling for further cutbacks.

The debate over the National Health Service was important, and the swift reaction of the Prime Minister and the Conservative Party chairman, Cecil Parkinson, to defuse the situation was a sign of what a hot political potato the leaked Think Tank report had become. But in a sense it diverted attention once again from the issue of the depressed state of the economy, and the need to change course. Here again, however, the Thatcherites came up with another red herring to draw across the track of the wets: 'It would take so long to bring unemployment down now,' they argued, 'that nothing we could do now would change things before a general election.'

The scale of the deflation administered under the Thatcher experiment was so formidable that even the most minute concessions offered by the government were greeted too effusively by those who were desperate for good news. The 1982 Budget, for instance – which, as we have seen, went down quite well in the Commons – contained a list of small measures aimed at helping business in some way. Indeed, ministers always seemed to be unveiling measures aimed at small businesses. But the small businesses were suffering from the same recession as the large businesses. Without a stimulus to overall demand, they could do precious little to provide an entrepreneurial revival. The 'costs' of the many measures to help businesses were listed as 'nil' or 'negligible', and this had obvious implications for the size of the benefits.

I argued in a previous book that, whatever the intentions of an incoming administration, something happens to force them off course. In the case of the Heath administration this something was the fear of social disorder on Clydeside, which prompted a telephone call from the Chief Constable of Glasgow to No. 10, and was an important factor behind the general change of policies. In the case of the Labour administration of 1974–79, the something was the sterling crisis of 1976, which effectively meant that control over economic policy was assumed for a time by the US administration, as the principal shareholder in the International Monetary Fund.

Many of Mrs Thatcher's plans certainly went haywire during 1979–83. After the initial tax cuts – whose principal assistance was in any case to the top income earners – the tax burden rose, so that even after the March 1983 Budget it was much higher than at the beginning. Extra financial assistance had to be given to British Steel, the National Coal Board, the railways, and British Leyland on a scale that made nonsense of Sir Keith Joseph's original ideas for 'not intervening'. But the extra taxes, and the financial assistance, were all corollaries of what became the main purpose of Mrs Thatcher's administration – the determination to stick to the broad thrust of the deflationary policies she found herself with.

In the desire not to be seen to be weakening – to be 'doing a Heath' – the Prime Minister and her Chancellor were prepared to raise taxes, despite their promises, when the wets' annual revolt meant that public spending looked like being higher than planned. They also failed repeatedly to meet the monetary targets which had been built up as the centre of the strategy. In the end their entire attention was devoted to one virility symbol – keep the public sector borrowing requirement as low as possible, whatever traditional or conventional economics suggested.

The industrial intervention in cases such as British Steel in 1980, widely interpreted as a U-turn at the time, was in fact the compensation needed for not doing a U-turn – for not relaxing monetary and fiscal policy so that the exchange rate should come down and more demand be pumped into the economy. There was a U-turn of sorts over exchange rate policy in 1981; but, as we have seen, the very Budget designed to get interest rates down and relieve pressure on the exchange rate involved a tightening of the fiscal squeeze. And when the exchange rate did begin to fall in the autumn, interest rates were hoisted sharply. The U-turn attempt was abandoned, and the objective became exchange rate stability. This meant that the exchange rate continued to be sharply overvalued by comparison with the position a few years earlier.

The overvaluation of the exchange rate has been a central theme of this book. But, unlike the case when a currency is declining rapidly and a sense of emergency is in the air, a 'crisis of strength' does not seem to concentrate minds so much. On the contrary, as we have seen, the strong exchange rate was, for a long time, rationalized as an act of God about which the government could do little. Given what the exchange rate was doing to the profitability and viability of industry, however, the government found itself having to help in those areas where it was directly responsible – the public sector – and connive at 'excessive' bank lending to the private sector (encouraged in certain cases by the Bank of England) in order to keep household industrial names from 'going under'.

Once again, the government was adept at producing excuses: the competitiveness problem took time to become fully apparent in the trade figures, and spokesmen were fond of statements such as 'exports are looking up well'. In fact the trade position deteriorated sharply; by the second quarter of 1982 Britain, the former workshop of the world, had become a net importer of manufactured goods. Competitiveness had become a definite constraint on expansion, to the point where the Treasury was arguing that it was no good reducing income tax, because half the money would be absorbed by imports.

The competitiveness problem posed by the high exchange rate, and the deflationary stance of fiscal policy, had contributed in large measure to a decline of over 5 per cent in gross domestic product over the period 1980 and 1981, and to the doubling of unemployment. The prospect of virtually no growth in the economy and unemployment going on up to 3 million – a prospect much enhanced by the stance of economic policy – was leading the dry ministers to redouble their efforts to cut public spending, because they saw it as an ever-rising proportion of a depressed GDP.

Yet it was the tame acceptance of this static position, and the belief on the part of evangelical ministers that they could do nothing about it, which was so puzzling. Public expenditure had helped both Britain and the US to emerge from the depression of the early 1930s. It was not as if, with 2 million and then 3 million and then 3½ million unemployed, and the majority of firms working well below capacity, there were no spare resources in the economy.

One of the most intriguing aspects of the Thatcher economic experiment has been the role of Mrs Thatcher herself. This book has been concerned specifically with the economy, but Prime Ministers, by definition, have other concerns besides the economy. The range of their interests, and their need to travel abroad frequently, means that traditionally Prime Ministers flit in and out of the economic policy discussions which are going on all the time within and between the Treasury and the Bank of England.

Few witnesses to the Thatcher experiment have any doubts that Mrs Thatcher imprinted more of her personality than most Prime Ministers on economic policy decisions. She was an extraordinarily dominant personality at all Cabinet and Cabinet committee discussions, running things in a dictatorial way which was not at all in keeping with ideals or recent memories of Cabinet government (ironically, the exception to this rule may have been certain stages of the administration of Edward Heath, the man she detested so much). She had come to power as a populist politician, expressing the deepest feelings – pro-hanging, anti-immigrant – of a large section of the British people. The story of most post-war governments had been one of Prime Ministers trying to act in accordance not necessarily with the reality, but with an ideal of what the British people thought and felt. Mrs Thatcher was different, and stayed different in office.

Mrs Thatcher's behaviour and manner are of only peripheral relevance to a book on the economy. But it is noteworthy that she took the cosy world of Whitehall and the Bank of England by storm, and offended many of the British rules of propriety about the way to talk to senior people in front of their juniors. It has also been suggested that she made up her mind about people within five seconds of meeting them. It was certainly quite a feat for her to develop such bad relations with both the head of the Treasury and the Governor of the Bank of England – presumably a ten-second job – although these were eventually patched up in the case of the former.

The conduct of economic policy is difficult enough without the additional handicap of bad personal relations between the major participants. It was said by some that Mrs Thatcher really wanted people to stand up to her – otherwise they were, in her favourite epithet, 'wet'. Yet it is equally true that some of the civil servants who did stand up to her found themselves frozen out. It seems that a subtle mixture of confidence, determination and sycophancy was required from officials.

We have already referred to the difficulties of the relationship between Mrs Thatcher and Gordon Richardson, who had been appointed Governor of the Bank of England by Edward Heath, and who was seen by the Thatcher camp as one of the men associated with the policies that led to the 1976 sterling crisis. Their exchanges became a running joke in Whitehall and Westminster. 'There is little that can be done about this,' said one observer. 'He is feline and she is canine.' But whatever the personal difficulties, the more substantial problem was that Richardson was in the classic position of the Greek messenger – the man who was forever delivering the bad news about the failure of the figures to comply with the dictates of pure monetarism. It did not help that, according to the Thatcher camp, Richardson had promised her early on that the Bank *would* be able to achieve the monetary targets – well before the emergence of the Bank's disbelief in M3 and all that, according to this camp.

Richardson was in a strong position, because short of convicting him of treason, there was little Mrs Thatcher could do to hurt him before his term came to a close in July 1983. Wet ministers, and critical back-benchers, were always at Mrs Thatcher's political mercy, and Treasury civil servants early latched on to the fact that the Thatcherites disliked civil servants as a breed, and that important promotions would depend on prime-ministerial favour as much as the views of their Civil Service seniors.

The only reprisal open to Mrs Thatcher in Richardson's case was not to offer him a further term. The Prime Minister devoted a fair amount of effort to looking for other candidates; one by one these scored black marks, and for a time there was a possibility that she might be forced to reappoint Richardson, at least for a short period. But this would have been considered too shameful an admission of defeat by a 'radical' Prime Minister, and in any case there was a desire for new blood within the Bank itself. Finally an acceptable outsider was found in the person of Robin Leigh-Pemberton, chairman of the Nat West clearing bank. (There was a public furore about the appointment, but at least he was acceptable to the Prime Minister.) Richardson was given a peerage, but not reappointed. There is one story about Richardson and Mrs Thatcher which is hardly pertinent to the conduct of monetarism but which does, as it were, help people to capture the flavour of everyday government under her. It is said that Mrs Thatcher would alternate between bouts of abuse against her officials and moments when motherly feelings would come to the surface, and tenderness prevail. On one afternoon the Governor, lord of all he surveyed in the parlours of Threadneedle Street, was being hectored at No. 10 about the failure of the Bank to control the monetary statistics. Suddenly, as it were, the match was stopped for a tea break. 'Gordon, you must have some of this delicious chocolate cake given to me by Mrs Gandhi.' 'No thank you, Prime Minister.' 'No, come on, you must.' The story relates that the Governor eventually conceded, and accepted the proffered cake with some disdain.

Throughout 1979–83 there was an interesting paradox behind judgements about her. Those who expected a U-turn at some stage were accustomed to say, 'She is a politician at heart. She wants to defeat inflation, but she also wants to win the election'. Yet major changes of approach were still not discernible by May 1983; indeed, primitive Thatcherism seemed to have been born again on the crest of the Falklands victory and the opinion polls of the summer of 1982.

The popular impression of Mrs Thatcher was that of a determined woman who knows her mind. The more private view of politicians and officials close to her was of someone much less certain, and often open to persuasion. But it is not difficult to reconcile these positions. Like so many – but not all – politicians, Mrs Thatcher wanted power above all else, and she wished to retain it. It is worth recalling the comment of one of her closest colleagues about the campaign promise to implement the Clegg settlements: 'She wanted to be Prime Minister like there was no tomorrow.'

There was a tomorrow, and one of the main themes of this book has been that, after the campaign promises and the first Budget, it *was* 'tomorrow'; and the government devoted most of its economic efforts to trying to repair 'today's' initial damage. In the process, though, they managed to inflict further damage.

Monetarism was a policy which both suited Mrs Thatcher's prejudices and offered, according to its ebullient salesmen, a miraculous cure for the ills of the British economy. When monetarism was seen to be flawed, Mrs Thatcher was prepared to acquiesce in decisions which did not accord with pure monetarism – for instance, to lower interest rates even when the money supply was expanding fast, and to agree, when the exchange rate was above $2.40, that it should be brought down.

These were 'pragmatic' decisions, the decisions of a typical politician. So were a spate of decisions from mid 1982 onwards – such as a freeze on certain nationalized industry prices – with an eye on the coming election. What was not pragmatic, however, was the stance of the overall economic policy, which continued to be heavily restrictive. Deep down, Mrs Thatcher must have been as convinced of her 'no alternative' assertions as, to judge from the opinion polls, a large proportion of the electorate seemed to be, even in May 1983, with unemployment at 3½ million.

Another story concerned the Prime Minister and a meeting with Treasury officials over whether or not government stock, which was indexed against inflation, should be issued to the general public. Mrs Thatcher's famous denunciations of people and views tended to be excused by her associates as 'testing an argument to its limits'. On this occasion she is said to have railed passionately against the high cost in interest charges of servicing the national debt. The government was being swindled by the City, she said. When it was pointed out to her that over the years the 'real value' of the debt had fallen, and the government had not done so badly, she immediately launched into a tirade against the government for swindling the public.

'There has never been a Prime Minister more interested in the economy and in the *details* of the economy,' said one of her colleagues. 'Can you imagine Macmillan inviting two foreign economists to No. 10 to explain the obscure details of monetary control?'

Sir Geoffrey Howe at No. 11 was said to be much more vacillating and indecisive on minor decisions than Mrs Thatcher. As one official put it: 'Sir Geoffrey spends a lot of time agonizing – some would say dithering – about decisions: Mrs Thatcher tends to listen to the arguments and say, "We could do A, B, or C; I think we should do C." ' But if Howe was indecisive about day-to-day decisions, and considered very much under the dominant influence of the Prime Minister, he was as indefatigably inflexible on the major questions of the thrust of macro-economic policy as Mrs Thatcher herself. Even when Samuel Brittan, one of the original influences on Howe's monetarism, had decided enough was enough and was advocating £5 billion of reflationary measures (summer 1982), Howe just wanted to press on with reductions in the PSBR that made little sense in such a depressed economy. Howe's doggedness at the Treasury complemented Mrs Thatcher's dominance over the Cabinet. 'The only man who really stood up to her in Cabinet was Lord Carrington, and now he's gone,' was one woeful comment from a wet. (And that 'standing up' was not over economic policy.)

One event which the wets always feared under the Thatcher experiment was social unrest as a result of high unemployment. This was feared by the evangelicals too, but for a different reason: it might upset their plans. Yet the riots at Toxteth, Brixton and Bristol came and went in the summer of 1981, without any major changes in policy – although specific measures were taken to alleviate the problems of those particular areas; the Prime Minister even tried to maintain in the Commons that unemployment was not one of the causes of the riots.

Thus none of the factors that might possibly change the course of economic policy had been sufficiently strong by spring 1983 actually to be effective. It looked as though the only factor which could bring such a change into operation was Mrs Thatcher herself – yet the avoidance of such a move was central to the task she had set herself.

The Thatcher administration came into office in May 1979 when inflation was around 10 per cent and the economy widely considered to be showing signs of relative decline. They promised to bring inflation down and to revitalize the economy. Their campaign posters made a particular point of the extent of unemployment at the time of the campaign

(1·3 million or 5¾ per cent unemployed; 'Labour isn't Working'). Revitalization was going to be achieved by tax and public expenditure cuts and less intervention in industry; the conquest of inflation by control of the money supply, or monetarism.

Partly as a result of commitments made in the heat of the campaign, and partly through reliance on a doctrine – monetarism – that was found wanting, the Thatcher administration presided over a rise in the inflation rate to 21.9 per cent in its first year of office. It devoted the next two and a half years to applying a fiscal squeeze which brought inflation back to the rate which had been inherited. Only during the fourth year did inflation come down below the inherited rate. And during the four years as a whole prices rose on average by over 50 per cent. Unemployment during this period was more than doubled to 3½ million, and manufacturing output fell by a fifth between the second quarter of 1979 and the last quarter of 1980, with no signs of recovery in 1981 or 1982, and the merest glimmer during the spring of 1983. Although the rate of inflation, and the level of interest rates, suggested that the economy was now back to square one, the lost output and the rise in unemployment left the economy far feebler.

While there was much talk about making industry more competitive, British industry actually became much less competitive, vis-à-vis its counterparts in other countries, as a result of the surge in its wage costs and the rise in exchange rate during the first eighteen months. Its profits were badly squeezed, and it reacted by cutting back stocks, closing factories, postponing investment plans and drastically shedding labour.

Because demand was so tightly squeezed at home, there was no source of entrepreneurial activity to take up the people who had been declared redundant. Because by the autumn 1982 there was also a world recession, there was no obvious sign of higher demand there. And because the cost and exchange rate structure made industry so uncompetitive, it was not going to be easy to fight for such extra business as eventually materialized – just as in 1979–82 the competitiveness problem had meant that British industry supplied a lower share of whatever demand there was, national and international.

During that period the total volume of imports of the countries which comprise Britain's export markets grew by nearly 12 per cent, but our actual shipments to these markets fell by 5 per cent. This hardly accorded with governmental claims that the problems of our industries were caused by recession elsewhere (*OECD Economic Outlook*, December 1982). On the good side, it was said that productivity was rising much faster than before, and that managers had rediscovered the right to manage: workforces were being more cooperative. The case here was simply not proven: the productivity calculations showed that employment had fallen far more than output; they did not say whether these gains were permanent, or what would happen during a recovery. There had also of course been productivity gains during the depression of the 1920s and 1930s, when the unions had also been cowed. Ironically, many labour relations experts attributed the difficult labour relations of the post-war years to the hardening attitudes in the thirties.

Although the world recession aggravates the problem of a trading nation such as Britain, it is simply not true that the rise in unemployment under the Thatcher experiment was caused by the world recession. During the three years 1979, 1980 and 1981, gross domestic product rose by 5¾ per cent in the seven major industrial countries (US, Japan, Germany, France, UK, Italy and Canada) but fell by 2½ per cent in the UK alone. Between 1979 and 1982 unemployment rose from 5.0 per cent to 8.9 per cent in those countries taken together, but from 5.7 per cent to 13.3 per cent in Britain. These differences were closely associated with the impact on British industry of the deterioration in competitiveness, and the more deflationary stance of economic policy.

Wembley Stadium holds 100,000 people. The *increase* in unemployment between 1979 and 1983 was 2 million — enough to fill twenty football stadiums the size of Wembley. Unemployment has reached unimaginable heights, under a party which devoted itself in the early post-war period to shaking off the pre-war jibe that it was the party of unemployment.

EPILOGUE

In a previous book about British economic policy (*Who Runs the Economy?*) I argued that there is a cycle in economic policy, just as there is – or used to be – a cyclical process at work in the economy itself. According to this theory, politicians typically come into office in Britain with incompatible manifesto commitments which do not add up and inevitably go wrong.

In the early stages, before the chickens have come home to roost, the Prime Minister and Chancellor are very powerful in economic policy. Sooner or later, however, something goes wrong – Edward Heath's U-turn of 1972; the Wilson /Callaghan government's sterling crisis of 1976 – and other influences come to the fore, such as the economic policy machine of the Treasury and Bank of England, or on occasion the International Monetary Fund. A distinguishing feature of the first Thatcher administration of 1979–83, however, was that in one key area it held on to the reins of economic power and did not budge: there was no U-turn in what became the central criterion of its macro-economic policy, namely its determination to keep public sector borrowing as low as possible, whatever the consequences for output and employment.

The agenda for economic policy making under the 1979–83 Thatcher administration was drawn up in No. 10 Downing Street, and there it stayed. This determination reflected a religious zeal, to describe which I have used the term 'economic evangelicalism'. Mrs Thatcher and her evangelical colleagues came into office with a specific economic objective – the revival of the British economy via lower inflation, a smaller public sector, and tax incentives – and specific means: monetarism, a new, or rather revived, and revivalist, economic doctrine.

The evangelicals believed passionately that they were right, and their dogmatic fervour brooked no criticism. They had discovered their god, and there could be no alternative within their scheme of things; atheism and agnosticism were ruled out by the faith – such doubters were not 'one of us'. The evangelicals talked with certainty when all they possessed was mystical revelation. They talked with certainty about the importance of controlling the money supply, and their ability to do so, when they were in no position to possess such certainty.

When the evangelicals found the links between the money supply and the economy were not quite what they believed, and not quite so easy to control, they redoubled their efforts to control one particular component of the money supply, namely the public sector borrowing requirement. Their failure to meet their monetary targets misled many critics into believing that they had made a U-turn. But the continued obsession with the PSBR ensured that there was no let-up in the savage fiscal squeeze inflicted on the economy.

The obsession with monetarism and M3 was sufficiently strong, and lasted sufficiently long, to do grave damage to the economy, not only by depressing demand, but also by making British industry so uncompetitive that it lost a significant share of total demand. Monetarism misled the government in two ways in this area: the evangelicals believed that monetarism would somehow ensure that the wages explosion of 1979–80 was not inflationary; and it prevented them from intervening to stop the crippling rise in the exchange rate in 1979–80.

The obsession with the PSBR was fomented not only by monetarism but also by its failure: the PSBR became the one thing the government found it could keep down. The obsession with the PSBR also derived from the generally anti-government-spending prejudices of the evangelicals, quite independently of the monetary relationships in which the PSBR figures so strongly. The commonplace that some public spending was wrong and wasteful became logically – i.e. illogically – transposed into the conclusion that all public spending and borrowing (except on defence, law and order, etc.) were, *a priori*, suspect.

Any student of government economic policy knows the importance of the financial markets, and how a 'strike' by the men who purchase government stock can force up interest rates. It may be objected that in this book I have underrated the importance of the markets.

Perhaps. But the point about the Thatcher administration's espousal of monetarism and its obsession with the PSBR was that power was handed over to the financial markets on a plate. It was not the financial markets which enthusiastically adopted the Medium Term Financial Strategy with its targets for progressively reducing the PSBR. The markets did not ask the government to do this. It was the evangelicals themselves. They *wanted* to do it.

I have called this book *Mrs Thatcher's Economic Experiment*, but in an important sense it was not an experiment at all. The word 'experiment' implies a willingness to observe, and to alter assumptions accordingly. As the evangelicals approached the June 1983 general election there was little evidence that they had changed their basic economic preoccupations; indeed, the theme of the manifesto was 'more of the same'.

The Thatcher experiment was foisted on an only half-suspecting public by a group of ideologues who did not fully understand what they were doing, at a time when the critics who did understand what they were doing were politically weak and felt intellectually battered.

The Thatcherites seized on a defunct economic doctrine, and dressed it in their own clothes. Just as there are always confidence tricksters ready to part people from their money, so there are always intellectual deceivers ready to fill a vacuum, and capitalize on people's innate sense of guilt, in the belief that they deserve what is coming to them. The economic evangelicals spotted an opening, and filled it. They asserted, but did not prove, that past attempts to manage the economy had failed; and they promised to concentrate on doing what governments *could* do – not raise output, or guarantee full employment, but control the money supply and the level of public sector spending and borrowing and leave the rest to the private sector. The private sector did not respond, however, because the methods chosen by the evangelicals made the economic outlook much worse, so that there was no incentive for it to respond.

The evangelicals failed in their monetarism: they could not control the money supply the way they promised; and the causal connection between the money supply and inflation which they believed in did not exist. But they did succeed in imposing a savage squeeze on the British economy, the like of which it had not experienced for fifty years.

They got away with it, first, because they had no effective opposition – under the British system a determined Prime Minister, with a comfortable working majority, is extremely powerful, *a fortiori*, when the opposition is as weak as Labour was in the period 1979–83; and, second, because they produced a series of promises and excuses which succeeded in fooling enough of the people enough of the time. These excuses ranged from the logically incorrect assertion that 'there is no alternative' to repeated assertions that 'recovery is just around the corner'. Towards the end they began to deceive even themselves with such promises: thus, while taking a pride in maintaining a strong economic squeeze, they seemed to think that relatively costless pre-electoral budgetary concessions would transform the economy.

The evangelicals were scornful of their critics – an attempt by 364 non-monetarist economists to point to a practicable alternative was laughed out of existence by the government propaganda machine. And they were helped by the worldwide spread of the deflationary disease, so that in 1983 it became virtually impossible for the layman to distinguish between the damage caused by British domestic economic policy and that caused by the world recession.

Towards the end they had so devalued the level of public economic debate that they stood at least a chance of convincing people that their policies had worked if there was the merest hint of an upturn in the economy, from however low a level, and notwithstanding the damage that had been done to British industry.

POSTSCRIPT

The Conservative Party did indeed win the general election of 9 June 1983, in spite of the level of unemployment. Under the British electoral system of 'first past the post' they won by what was generally described as a landslide majority (144 seats), even though their share of the total vote was lower than when Edward Heath lost to Harold Wilson in 1966. One of the most notable features of the election was that the economy, and the economic record of the evangelicals, hardly featured in the campaign.

The election was dominated, if that is the word, by the debilitated state of the opposition. With the anti-government vote split between Labour and the SDP /Liberal Alliance, it was obvious from the beginning of the campaign that the Conservatives were in a commanding position. All the opinion polls told them this. The only matter in question was the size of the majority, and the campaign began with the leaders of *all* the parties knowing this.

The disarray of the Labour Party had given birth to the Alliance, but Labour had such a strong grip over its traditional strongholds in the north that the Alliance could not hope to win more than a handful of seats. During the campaign Labour's disarray was a far bigger talking point than the state of the economy. Whatever else they had not achieved, the evangelicals had timed the date of the poll to perfection.

The ministers who had played the most prominent role in the choice of the election date got their reward. Sir Geoffrey Howe was given the job he most coveted, namely the Foreign Secretaryship. Mr Cecil Parkinson, the party chairman, was made Secretary for a combined Trade and Industry Department. (He resigned in October for personal reasons and was succeeded by Norman Tebbit.) Mr Francis Pym, a wet who had been Foreign Secretary since Carrington's resignation, and who had never got on with the Prime Minister, had also been rash enough to say during the campaign that landslide majorities were not necessarily a good thing for the British parliamentary system. He was sent to the back benches. James Prior was kept at the Northern Ireland Office; Peter Walker, who had advised the Prime Minister to a certain extent on political tactics during the campaign, was given the Energy portfolio. One observer commented: 'It's like the Agatha Christie story: now there are two . . .'

Both Howe and Parkinson had argued forcefully against Mrs Thatcher when, at a meeting at Chequers at the beginning of May, she had expressed her intention of ignoring the pressure building up in the party for a June election, and of carrying on. One of the principal considerations in their minds was the belief that they should go 'while the going was good'. The opinion polls showed them the way ahead; the Labour Party would not have time to jettison their leader Michael Foot – who was generally considered by Tories and Labour men alike to be an electoral liability; furthermore, the Treasury's forecasts showed that unemployment was bound to get worse. Parkinson, though well in with the evangelical ministers, was one of those who shared the view of the wets that the unemployment issue could explode in the government's face at any moment.

Mrs Thatcher's second administration got off to a bad start in general. The debate on hanging and the proposals for a large increase in MPs' pay were handled ineptly. While the Prime Minister's need for a retina operation reminded people of her mortality, No. 10 Downing Street's handling of the news surrounding the operation left it looking nakedly untruthful. There was just a suggestion that the Thatcher entourage was beginning to lose its magic touch.

This was also true on the economic front. The new Chancellor, Nigel Lawson, had not been popular with the now depleted ranks of the wets (when stronger and more numerous they had successfully opposed his being given Cabinet rank). He now early established an abrasive style – and incurred considerable unpopularity – by attempting to 'bounce' his Cabinet colleagues into yet another round of public expenditure cuts at the beginning of July. The justification for these cuts was that spending for the 1983–84 financial year was running above forecast. He proposed £500 million off expenditure totals, and £500 million in extra 'privatization' proposals – selling more of the government's assets in the energy sector.

The episode served to confirm suspicions that the March 1983 Budget had been based on flagrantly 'electoral' arithmetic, in that the contingency reserve had been set unusually low and an ambitious assumption made about the degree to which government departments would 'underspend' the following year. Lawson made himself no more popular with his colleagues when he also revealed that the public sector borrowing figures had, in fact, been running on target during the first quarter of the 1983–84 financial year, so why the panic?

But in July 1983 the wets – or such wets as were left – felt as constrained as ever. Although they knew that the economy had hardly entered the election debate, the Prime Minister and her evangelical colleagues were still able to claim: 'These are the kinds of policies that won us the election.'

The unemployment figures for July showed another sharp rise: this confirmed, in a macabre sort of way, the feelings of the ministers who had urged that June was 'the right time to go' and of those wets who thought the economic – and potential social – situation was nowhere near amelioration.

To anyone who believed, in common with this author, that the economic experiment of the first Thatcher administration had taken the economy nowhere but down, the key questions as Thatcher Mark Two got under way were: first, would the experiment, in the face of all the evidence to the contrary, suddenly produce miraculous results at some time from now on? If not – and the whole tenor of this book shows my scepticism on this point – would there be a change of policy? Or would the rest of the world, in the event of no major change, nevertheless pull the British economy out of recession, and transform the unemployment situation?

Taking this last point first, one could see no obvious (or, for that matter, hidden) sign that the world was going to come to our rescue. Although there were strong signs of economic recovery in the US during the summer of 1983, the effects of this on our export demand were already taken into account in the July 1983 forecasts of the OECD, which still envisaged only a slow growth in UK output, and no change of direction in the unemployment trend. As for Europe, which is equally important to the UK as an export market, the forecasts were of very sluggish growth in output, and rising unemployment.

What about a change of policy? There was little to indicate any such intention on the part of the Prime Minister in her choice of Nigel Lawson as Chancellor. We have seen that Lawson was the major political force behind the MTFS as Financial Secretary to the Treasury in 1980. Lawson had in the past worked for both Sir Alec Douglas-Home and Edward Heath, and there were those in the Treasury who thought he might, in spite of his recent prominence as an evangelical, prove more flexible in the future than his recent reputation indicated.

There was little, however, in the early months of the second Thatcher administration to corroborate this theory. On the contrary: Lawson dug himself in fast. (One of Lawson's colleagues commented: 'Sir Geoffrey Howe used to call for endless papers and then be slow to come to a decision; Lawson asks for little and makes up his mind in advance.')

The welfare state in general, and the health service in particular, had come briefly into the debate during the election campaign, when the Think Tank report which had first surfaced during the Conservative conference of October 1982 was again leaked. Mrs Thatcher and her colleagues once again rushed to assert that the report on possible cuts in the welfare state was a discussion document which had been shelved. But the impression given by Lawson within a month of the election result was that it had been brought down from the shelf and dusted off. A theme emerging from the Conservative Conference in October was that the evangelicals had achieved enough, and that they should, in what became a vogue word, 'consolidate'. John Biffen was a leading proponent of this view. But within days of his autumn statement on public expenditure the new Chancellor went on television to say he did not wish to consolidate: he wanted to go a lot further in the attack on public spending, not least in the health service and social security.

The general tenor of the argument coming from the new Chancellor was that the country could not 'afford' its commitment to the welfare state. This argument was not put forward in the context of a fully employed economy where, for example, commitments to new hospital building or equipment from the public purse might be competing with the private sector for spare resources.

The argument seemed to lead ministers into what might be called a 'low growth trap'. If, said the evangelicals, economic growth was sluggish over the following few years, then either taxes would have to rise, or public expenditure be cut, in order that the PSBR could be contained, both absolutely and as a proportion of gross domestic product.

To a Keynesian way of thinking this almost guaranteed the perpetuation of low growth. The economy was already being held back by a fiscal squeeze; in the absence of a major change of policy, the slow growth feared by ministers and postulated in the Think Tank paper was, as it were, built into the system. To respond by threatening a further fiscal squeeze appeared perverse, to say the least – although it has to be recalled that such perversity was at the heart of evangelical economics.

In the pre-evangelical days pre-Thatcherites used to look at the underlying growth of productive potential in the economy (output per man, plus any additions to the labour force), and note that, unless output rose by some 2½ per cent a year (say), unemployment would rise. They would then look at the various components of demand – consumer spending, current spending by the public sector, exports (net of imports), investment (public and private) – and see what was forecast under existing policies. If there was too much pressure on resources, restrictive measures would be proposed; if there were spare resources, and the forecast was of low growth, then a stimulus would be called for. Such days were now gone.

In his autumn statement Mr Lawson was able to boast that the economy had been expanding at 3 per cent per annum during 1983, and a similar rate of growth was forecast for 1984. Lawson claimed that this 'recovery' was directly attributable to the Budget of 1981 when, as we saw earlier, the government opted for an 'unthinkably' low PSBR. Keynesians simply could not see this causal relationship. There had been two elements in this mild revival: first, the point had inevitably been reached where industry had run down its stocks to such an extent that more of existing demand was being met from new production; second, as the Bank of England pointed out in its Bulletins during 1983, consumer spending had received a boost from a sharp rise in bank lending and mortgage finance (much of the latter being devoted to the purchase of consumer durables).

This rise in consumer debt was the counterpart of a sharp fall in the proportion of incomes saved. It is, as we saw earlier, a standard part of the Keynesian analysis that a fall in savings will give a temporary boost to the economy. As 1983 drew to a close, the problem was that few forecasters could see a significant fall in unemployment emerging from the growth rates being forecast; and the exchange rate was still relatively high.

The economic policies of the second Thatcher administration therefore bore marked resemblances to those of the first, at least in the early stages. Would they enjoy quite such an easy ride as in the previous four years? Or would people wake up to the possibility that the rewards held out by the economic evangelicals, like those promised by their religious forebears, were perhaps not of this world after all? One could not but think that at some stage there would be a political reaction. It was fashionable after the June 1983 election result, and amid continuing disarray in the opposition, to say that Mrs Thatcher would be in office indefinitely. But it should also perhaps have been borne in mind that there had eventually been a political reaction to the economic policies of the 1920s and 1930s, even if this had not taken place until 1945. Which was where we came in . . .

November 1983

GLOSSARY

DEMAND, DEMAND MANAGEMENT The words 'demand' and 'supply' are fundamental to economics. Basic textbooks contain diagrams illustrating how the demand for, say, potatoes, will fall if the price rises (there may be a switch to bread or pasta) and so on. More usually these days, however, the word 'demand' on its own is used to refer to the demand for all the goods and services produced in the country – or rather 'demanded' in the country.

'Demand management' is the traditional Keynesian method of trying to keep the economy on an even keel by changing taxes and public expenditure in order to affect the level of economic activity and employment in the country. 'Demand' is aggregate expenditure: consumer spending (which accounts for about half of total expenditure); current spending by the public sector; investment (public and private); and exports (net of imports, which of course do not directly affect employment in the UK).

ECONOMICS From the Greek οἶκος, meaning household. Running the affairs of the household. For Adam Smith (1776) the subject was an inquiry into the causes of the wealth of nations. The market place is central to economics – explaining the supply and demand for a product, and the relationship of the so-called 'factors of production' – capital, labour, raw materials – which go into its production. In the nineteenth and early twentieth centuries economists were much concerned with how production could be maximized, and how it was best distributed. These preoccupations did not disappear – the degree to which taxes and public spending should be used to redistribute income have remained a major political issue between left and right. During the great depression, however, the predominant issue became how to achieve FULL EMPLOYMENT. Classical economists argued that, left to itself, the market would find equilibrium (a favourite economists' word). KEYNES and his followers argued that equilibrium would not necessarily be reached at full employment; government could and should intervene, through lower taxes and higher spending, to boost the demand for output and hence employment. These policies were widely pursued from the end of the Second World War in 1945 until the 1970s, when INFLATION took over as the major policy preoccupation, and employment suffered as a result. (MONETARISTS justified this change of priorities by arguing that in the long run the defeat of inflation and greater freedom for the market place were a prerequisite of restoring full employment.)

FISCAL POLICY The principal Keynesian tool for the management of the demand for goods and services in the economy. Tax cuts will put more money into people's pockets, expand demand, and raise employment. So will higher spending by the government on public works for social security payments. But when the economy is fully employed or 'overheated' – it seems a long time ago – the brake can be applied by raising taxes and cutting public spending. The extraordinary contribution of the Thatcher government was to reverse the normal Keynesian procedure, and to cut public spending and raise the tax burden when the economy was already in recession.

FULL EMPLOYMENT Not what it sounds, but a long way from what we have recently experienced. There is always a small hard core of people who for one reason or another do not want to work or are unemployable. However busy the country's factories and offices are, there will always be some unemployment: even at the peak of a boom, a firm may decide to move to another area, and those who cannot go with it – because of school and family ties – will be temporarily unemployed until they find a new job that appeals to them. In any one year there are new entrants from schools and colleges to the labour force, and these may be unemployed for a time. Moreover some areas of the country – for example the south-east of England – are always busier than areas with industries in decline. Thus, even in the boom years of the 1950s and 1960s, 'full employment' in practice meant 'very low unemployment' – of around 2 per cent.

Even this figure rose over the years. By the 1970s it was found that higher unemployment benefits and the introduction of redundancy payments enabled people to spend longer searching for new jobs. This pushed up the average level of unemployment at any one time, so that 'full employment' might now mean, perhaps, a situation where 4 per cent of the labour force was unemployed. This, however, is a very long way from the rate of 13 per cent experienced in the early 1980s, when it was pre-eminently clear that the vast majority of the unemployed were unemployed because there was no work for them however long they searched.

INFLATION A sustained rise in the *average* level of prices. There have always been rises in some prices, even during years of severe depression. Prices essentially reflect supply and DEMAND – apples are cheaper in summer, and in years of plenty. Pricing policies take into account both the costs of production – wages, raw materials, transport – and desired profit. Profits will be all the greater if the product is in short supply, or the supplier has a monopoly position. The classic definition of inflation is 'too much money chasing too few goods': that was certainly the position after the First World War in Germany, where, with production devastated and bank notes plentiful, inflation reached rates of 1,000 per cent per week and there were jokes about the need for a wheelbarrow of notes in order to buy a loaf of bread. When production is reasonably normal, however, and the central bank is trying to gear the level of bank advances and the note issue to the needs of the economy, that sort of 'demand inflation' is much less in evidence. Then the real trouble comes from cost pressures, which naturally lead manufacturers to mark up their prices. The rises in the price of oil in the 1970s were inflationary in the sense that they pushed up the average price level; but oil, though important, was only a small part of total costs. The biggest cost pressure in the 1970s came from wage demands which were excessive in the sense that they could only be granted if employers passed them on in inflationary price rises. But even during periods of rapid increase in the average price level, some prices are falling as a result of technological progress and competition between manufacturers: a good example in the 1970s was the pocket calculator, first sold at £70 or more, and eventually at only a few pounds.

INTEREST RATES The rate of interest is the price paid for money, or the return for lending it, depending on your standpoint. Keynes explained the rate of interest as 'the reward for parting with liquidity'. The 'nominal' interest rate is the rate usually quoted; the 'real' interest rate is the rate after allowing for inflation. The rate is clearly affected by whether or not it is liable to tax. The feature of the Thatcher experiment was the long period when both nominal and real interest rates were high. And even when nominal rates came down during 1982 the real rate remained high, because the rate of inflation was also falling. Changes in interest rates are the key weapon of MONETARY POLICY. They can operate not only directly, but indirectly: if interest rates in London are higher than in other countries, foreign funds are attracted to London, the demand for the pound rises, and the exchange rate goes up. This was an important feature of the way monetary policy operated in Britain in 1979–82: it meant that British industry was squeezed not only by the direct cost of funds, but also by the fact that the high exchange rate made its goods less competitive, in relation to the goods of foreign producers, in both home and export markets.

KEYNES, John Maynard (1883–1946) The great Cambridge economist, who gave his name to what are known as KEYNESIAN policies. His central insight was that national economics was different from household economics. When, during a slump, a government such as the National Government of 1931 tried to raise taxes or cut unemployment benefit in order to balance its books, it only made matters worse, by reducing further the spending power of the nation. The great

Glossary

puritanical instinct to *save* more could exacerbate the slump by withdrawing yet more spending power. Much has been heard under Mrs Thatcher's administration of the need to avoid 'printing money'; Keynes argued that if people and resources were idle, it made sense to print more money and lower its price (the *rate of interest*). This would not lead to a classic INFLATION (too much money chasing too few goods); the counterpart to the extra money would be the new goods produced through a relaxed monetary policy. In addition to lower interest rates the way to create what Keynes called this extra *effective demand* was to lower taxes and raise government spending – the reverse of the economic orthodoxy of the time. It is important to remember that Keynes's analysis was essentially for a 'closed economy' – problems were to arise if countries tried to pursue Keynesian policies when other countries, and holders of money, had no confidence in them. Keynes was also more concerned with getting an economy back to full employment than with *economic growth*, or the pursuit of the fastest possible growth rate. And he lived in a world where there were less worries than now about energy shortages.

KEYNESIANS Followers of, and builders on, the work of Keynes. The rearmament programme had helped the British economy to recover from the slump in the late 1930s. And the economy was fully employed during the war. Keynes and his followers worked during the war to ensure that there would not be a repetition of the slump which had followed the 1914–18 war. The other half of the pump-priming policies to ensure FULL EMPLOYMENT was the need to apply a foot on the brake if the economy showed signs of 'overheating' and of inflationary pressure (a position of what became known as 'overfull employment'). Then Keynesian policies required higher taxes, a rise in interest rates, and lower government spending, in order to redress the balance.

Success with Keynesian full employment led to ambition for higher things – not just full employment, but faster economic growth, so that distribution problems would be easier if there was more to distribute. The desire for this was manifested in the high *wage demands* which were seen by Keynesians as the major engine of inflation. Although the danger of accelerating inflation was considered ever-present, the kind of pressures experienced in the 1950s and 1960s were as nothing compared to those of the 1970s. Keynesians thought these could be coped with by way of *incomes policies*.

MONETARISM The belief that control of the MONEY SUPPLY is both a necessary and sufficient condition for controlling inflation. The high priest of monetarism is Professor Milton Friedman, late of Chicago University, who claimed in a monumental work to have established a correlation between changes in the money supply in the US and subsequent changes in the price level. Friedman's analysis was never accepted by Keynesians such as James Tobin for the US itself – the main criticism being that cause and effect was never established, and that more rapid growth of the money supply could merely be a reflection of more deep-seated inflationary pressures. Friedman then proceeded to apply his US findings to the world in general and found willing disciples in Britain, where the manifestation of greater inflationary pressures in the late 1960s and early 1970s was leading some Keynesians to lose their faith in what had by now become the conventional wisdom – viz. the belief that governments had the power to control the level of demand for goods and services in the economy, and that wage inflation demanded specific *incomes policies*. Monetarism in Britain became associated with the school that disbelieved in the efficacy of *demand management*. Keynesians argued that it was difficult to control the money supply; that this was not the right objective if you were trying to control inflation; and that sole reliance on monetary policy might lead to excessively high interest rates with damaging consequences to the economy. They felt they were never given satisfactory answers by the monetarists to the question, 'What is the mechanism by which controlling the money supply controls inflation?'

MONETARY POLICY The government, through the Bank of England, is a powerful force in the financial market place, if only because it is such a big spender and borrower. It can, through its purchases and sales of securities, influence the liquidity of the banking system, and hence the growth of bank advances. The primary route is via the rate of interest – making credit cheaper or more expensive. One of the essential differences between Keynesians and monetarists concerns their respective degree of emphasis on monetary policy. For much of the post-war period – the heyday of the Keynesian consensus policies – monetary policy was seen as only one weapon in the armoury; once the decision had been made that the bias should always be in favour of cheap money, Keynesians tended to regard FISCAL POLICY as a more important weapon in general stabilization policy. But it was always recognized that excessively tight monetary policies would damage the economy. Monetarists cited the damage done by tight money and high real INTEREST RATES between the wars as evidence of the power of monetary policy, when criticizing the efficacy of fiscal policy and DEMAND MANAGE-MENT generally in more recent years. But fiscal policies were also tight between the wars – there was a similar obsession with balanced budgets and cutting the PSBR. And, as we have seen, under the Thatcher experiment monetarism actually operated via very tight fiscal policies.

MONEY SUPPLY One of the problems with monetarism is the wide variety of measurements for the money supply. The narrow 'monetary base' comprises largely notes and coins in circulation, but is only a small fraction of the spending power available to the economy, which comes principally through bank credit. Wider definitions include notes and coins plus bank deposits (M3), plus building society deposits (PSL2, or Private Sector Liquidity). M3, chosen as the target to be controlled by the Thatcher government, proved a very misleading guide to the course of inflation: shortly before inflation began to fall sharply, the M3 figures suggested it would accelerate. This confirmed Keynesian doubts about the whole business. They always knew that inflation could be brought down if the government created a big enough slump. But influential monetarists had promised that controlling the money supply offered a kind of philosopher's stone, which would defeat inflation at minimal cost to output and employment.

PUBLIC SECTOR BORROWING REQUIREMENT What all branches of government need to borrow each year to make up for the spending that cannot be financed from taxation. Keynesians argue that it is very proper for the PSBR to expand during a recession, to offset the contractionary effect of lower tax receipts and higher social security disbursements. The same applies to excessive savings by the private sector – the government may need to give a temporary boost to its own spending to mitigate the contractionary effects of this.

There is a definitional link between M3 and the PSBR, in that changes in M3 reflect the combination of a rise in bank advances to the private sector, and the public sector borrowing requirement. M3 is also affected by the balance of payments, rising when there is a net inflow of foreign exchange into the country, and *vice versa*. To the extent that the PSBR is funded by sales of long-term government stock ('gilts') it is paid for by savings, and does not involve the creation of 'new money' (raising 'M3') by the banking system. This PSBR/M3 link caused added emphasis to be placed on the alleged need to cut the PSBR under the Thatcher administration – in order to control M3 when the government was unable to control bank lending – and provided the monetary route to a tight FISCAL POLICY.

INDEX

Index

Index

Index

Index

Index

Index

Index

concern over public
spending, 80

concern over state
encroachment, 80

espousal of economic
evangelicalism, 81–2,
199–200, 206–7

influence of 1972–3 events
on, 55

interest and involvement in
economy, 118, 133, 134,
135, 136, 196–201

personality of, 134–5,
196–201 passim

populism of, 67–8, 134, 197

president of Centre for Policy
Studies, 46

reaction to Niehans study,
160

relationship with Bank of
England, 150–54, 155

second administration,
209–14

sessions with monetarist
economists, 125–6, 153–4

speeches and thinking
(1975–79), 76

views on public spending, 82

views on *The Right
Approach to the Economy*,
104

Think Tank deliberations
(1982), 193

Thorneycroft, Peter (Lord
Thorneycroft)

made Conservative Party
chairman, 70

removed from chairmanship,
172–3

resignation (1958), 21, 70,
173

Times, The, 41, 43, 50, 52, 60,
79, 91

prints Joseph's Preston
speech, 49

Toxteth riots (1981), 201

Trades Union Congress (TUC),
20

and 'Social Contract', 78

Treasury, 80, 126, 205

all-party select committee on,
185

and exchange rate (1979–81),
163–4

attitude to monetarism (after
1976), 88

economic advice from, 184

model of the economy, 45

November 1982 statement,
180

reaction to 1981 Budget, 169

relationship with Bank of
England, (1980–81), 154,
158

Trade unions

and Heath government,
29–30, 31, 32, 73

and Thatcher government
(1979–83), 112–15

attempts at reform (1964–74),
20–30

cowed by monetarist
policies, 114

economic evangelicals' view
of, 77, 78, 79

government concessions to
(1974–79), 78

growth in wage bargaining
influence, 58

monopolistic powers of, 115

Tories' relationship with, 67,
103, 112–13

Tory policy on (1976–79), 103